D0912148

THE GENERAL PUBLIC'S GUIDE TO

NEW JERSEY WILLS,

ESTATES, TAXES

AND PLANNING

9th Edition 2005

by

Robert G. Saliba

Member, New Jersey Bar

authorHOUSE™

1663 LIBERTY DRIVE, SUITE 200
BLOOMINGTON, INDIANA 47403
(800) 839-8640
WWW.AUTHORHOUSE.COM

First published by AuthorHouse 09/28/05

ISBN: 1-4208-6948-5 (sc)

Printed in the United States of America
Bloomington, Indiana

This book is printed on acid-free paper.

AUTHOR'S NOTE

When this book was first published in 1984, I did not anticipate its popularity. Nor did I anticipate that the continuous heavy demand for it would discourage me from retiring it. So here's the 9th edition, all revised.

This book is my personal response to the intense curiosity and gross misinformation I have encountered in over thirty-eight years of law practice.

The General Table of Contents is as follows:

A more detailed Table of Contents begins on the page v.

Many, but not all, areas are covered. This is not a do-it-yourself kit with forms. The estate area is too complicated for that. Nor is it a sales pitch as to what people should do with their affairs (there is no law that says you have to have a will); however, there is some advice on seeking assistance from qualified professionals.

This book is intended to be a helpful, educative guide. But: there is no substitute for competent professional advice.

ROBERT G. SALIBA, ESQ.
One Western Avenue
Morristown, NJ 07960
(973)-538-0060

TABLE OF CONTENTS

PART I:
DYING WITHOUT A WILL

1. What Happens When You Die Without a Will?

If you die without a will, you die **intestate**. Your estate is administered and distributed in accordance with the New Jersey law.

First - and this happens if you die with or without a will – assets **not subject to administration** go to the named beneficiary or survivor. Some common examples of assets not subject to administration include:

A home in the joint names of you and another with the right of survivorship.

A bank account in the joints names of you and another with right of survivorship or in your name and payable to another upon your death.

A life insurance policy that names another as beneficiary.

A company pension plan or individual retirement account that names another as beneficiary.

In all the above examples the beneficiary or survivor automatically takes your entire interest in the asset. There is no administration.

If the beneficiary or survivor in any of the above examples dies before you do and there is no successor beneficiary or survivor named, then the beneficiary could be your estate. The property would not pass outside administration but would be part of the intestate estate. The following discussion concerns the distribution of assets which do not fall into the above category – assets which are subject to administration.

2. *When You Die Without a Will and Leave A Surviving Spouse*

1. Your spouse takes your entire estate if you leave no parents or no descendants (children, grandchildren and the like).

2. Your spouse takes your entire estate if all your surviving descendants are also your spouse's and your spouse leaves no surviving descendants (your spouse's children, who would be your step-children).

3. Your spouse takes the first 25% of your estate (but not less than $50,000.00 nor more than $200,000.00) plus 75% of the balance of your estate if you leave no descendants but you do leave parents. Your parents (or the survivior of them) take the remaining 25% of your estate.

4. Your spouse takes the first 25% of your estate (but not less than $50,000.00 nor more than $200,000.00) plus 50% of the balance of your estate if

    a. All your surviving descendants are yours and your spouse's and your spouse has one or more descendants who are not yours (your spouse's children, who would be your step-children). Your descendants (but not your spouse's descendants) take the remaining 50% of your estate, or

b. One or more of your surviving descendants (such as your child, who is your surviving spouse's step-child) is <u>not</u> <u>your</u> <u>surviving</u> <u>spouse's</u>. Your descendants (not your spouse's) take the remaining 50% of your estate.

3. When You Die Without A Will and Do Not Leave A Surviving Spouse

1. Your <u>descendants</u> take your <u>entire</u> <u>estate</u> *by Representation.* ("By Representaton" will be discussed at Page 5).

2. If you leave <u>no</u> <u>surviving</u> <u>descendants</u>, your <u>parents</u> (or the survivor of them) take your <u>entire</u> <u>estate</u>.

3. If you leave <u>no</u> <u>surviving</u> <u>descendants</u> or <u>parents</u>, then your <u>parents'</u> <u>descendants</u> take your <u>entire</u> <u>estate</u> <u>by representation</u>. (Your parents' descendants would be your brothers, sisters, nieces, nephews, etc).

4. If you leave <u>no</u> <u>surviving</u> <u>descendants</u> or <u>parents</u> or <u>parents'</u> <u>descendants</u>, but you do leave one or more <u>grandparents</u>, then:

    a. Your <u>paternal</u> <u>grandparents</u> (or the survivor of them) take 50% of your estate. However, if you leave no surviving grandparents but you do leave surviving a maternal grandparent or grandparents, then your paternal grandparents' descendants (such as the cousins) take 50% of your estate.

    b. Your <u>maternal</u> <u>grandparents</u> (or the survivor of them) take 50% of your estate. However, if you leave no surviving maternal grandparents but you do leave surviving a paternal grandparent or grandparents, then your maternal grandparents' descendants (such as the cousins) take 50% of your estate.

5. If you leave <u>no</u> surviving <u>descendants</u> or <u>parents</u> or parents' <u>descendants</u> or <u>grandparents</u>, then your <u>grandparents' descendants</u> take your estate.

6. If you leave no surviving descendants or parents or parents' descendants or grandparents or grandparents' descendants, then your step-children or their descendants take your entire estate, and if there are none of these, ***then there is no one who may inherit your estate***.

If there is no one who may inherit your estate, then your entire estate goes to the State of New Jersey. This is technically known as "Escheat." Your estate ***escheats*** to the State. To summarize:

IF YOU DIE WITHOUT A WILL AND LEAVE A SURVIVING SPOUSE:

No parents <u>or</u> descendants.	Spouse takes all.
Descendants of you and your spouse <u>and</u> no descendants of your spouse.	Spouse takes all.
No descendants <u>but</u> you do leave parents.	Spouse takes first 25% (not less than $50,000 or more than $200,000) and 75% of the balance <u>and</u> the parents take the rest.
Descendants of you and your spouse <u>and</u> descendants of your spouse <u>or</u> descendants of you <u>but</u> <u>not</u> of your spouse.	Spouse takes the first 25% (not less than $50,000 or more than $200,000) and 50% of the balance <u>and</u> your descendants take the rest.

4

IF YOU DIE WITHOUT A WILL AND LEAVE NO SURVIVING SPOUSE:

If you leave...	Then...
Descendants.	Descendants take all by representation.
No descendants but parents.	Parents or the survivor of them take all.
No descendants or parents.	Your parents' descendants take all by representation.
No descendants or parents or parents' descendants.	Your Paternal grandparents take 50% and your maternal grandparents take 50%. See more detailed discussion above.
No descendants or parents or parents' descendants or grandparents.	Your grandparents' descendants take all.
No descendants or parents or parents' descendants or grandparents or grandparents' descendants.	Your step-children or their descendants take all and if none, then the State of New Jersey takes all.

4. Descendants "Take By Representation"

When your descendants are not equally related to you, they take by representation. The following example might be the best way to explain the "by representation" concept.

Suppose you die widowed (having survived your spouse) and are survived by two children and two grandchildren. The two grandchildren are those of a third child of yours who died before you did. Your estate is divided into three shares. Your two surviving children each take one share and your two surviving grandchildren take the third share equally.

Now suppose you die widowed (having survived your spouse) and are survived by one child and three grandchildren. Two grandchildren are those of one child of yours who died before you did, and the other grandchild is that of another child of yours who died before you did.

Your estate is divided into three shares. The one surviving child takes one share. The other two shares are divided equally between your three surviving grandchildren. This is taking *by representation.*

Taking by representation replaces **per stirpes**. To explain per stirpes, you take the last examples in which you are survived by one child and three grandchildren, two grandchildren from one deceased child of yours and the other grandchild from another deceased child of yours. Your estate is divided into three shares. The one surviving child takes one share. The two surviving grandchildren of the one predeceased child of yours take one share equally, and the other surviving grandchildren of the other predeceased child of yours takes one share.

Taking *per capita* (if you have heard of that term) would be when your surviving descendants take everything in equal shares.

If you die without a will, your descendants take by representation.

5. *Survivorship: The 120 Hour Rule*

Any person who is entitled to inherit all or part of your estate when you die without a will must survive you by 120 hours (5 days). If such person does not, he or she shall be deemed to have died before you did.

If the times of death of you and your heir cannot be determined by clear and convincing evidence, your heir is deemed not to have survived for the 120 hours.

For example, you and your heir go mountain climbing, and your bodies are discovered a month later. It cannot be determined who died first or, if you did die first, how long your heir survived. Your heir is deemed not to have survived you for 120 hours.

> Note: This rule of law will not be applied if the result would cause your estate to pass to the State of New Jersey.

6. Additional Points

1. A relative of the half blood inherits the same share he or she would inherit if he or she were of the whole blood.

2. An individual in gestation (conceived but unborn) at a particular time who lives at least 120 hours (5 days) after birth is treated as living at that particular time.

3. A lawfully adopted child or adult inherits the same as if he or she were a natural child of the decedent.

4. A child born out of wedlock is the child of its natural parents regardless of their marital status.

5. A person is not disqualified to be an heir because he or she is or has not at any prior time been a United States citizen.

7. Administration When You Die Without A Will

Administration is the legal procedure which takes place from the time of your death until your estate is finally distributed to the person or persons entitled to it.

Administration takes place in the County in which you died a resident. The court which has jurisdiction is usually the Surrogate's Court, which deals with estate administration. The Superior Court of New Jersey, Chancery Division, Probate Part, also has jurisdiction.

When you die without a will the Court appoints an **Administrator**. The Administrator collects and preserves your assets, pays your debts and your taxes, and finds your heirs and distributes your estate to them.

8. Is Administration Always Required?

No. If you leave a surviving spouse and the total value of your property does not exceed $20,000.00, your spouse shall be absolutely entitled to all your property without administration. *If you leave no surviving spouse but you do leave surviving an heir or heirs*, and the total value of your property does not exceed $10,000.00, your heir or heirs shall be absolutely entitled to all your property without administration.

The procedure which is then followed in the Court is **Affidavit in Lieu of Administration**, which is signed by the surviving spouse or heir, as the case may be, and recites that the value of the estate does not exceed $20,000.00 or $10,000.00, as the case may be, your residence at the time of your death, the names, residences, and relationship of all of your heirs and the nature, location and value of your real property and personal property.

9. What Are Letters of Administration And To Whom Are They Granted?

Letters of Administration are legal documents issued by the Surrogate to the Administrator of your estate. They authorize and empower the Administrator to administer your estate. Certified copies of Letters of Administration are used along with other documents to do such things as open estate bank accounts and sell or transfer estate assets.

If you die without a will, Letters of Administration are granted to your surviving spouse.

If your surviving spouse will not accept administration or if you do not have a surviving spouse, then either or all of your heirs may be granted Letters of Administration if they will accept them.

If none of your heirs will accept administration, then Letters of Administration will be granted to any person who accepts administration.

If you die leaving no spouse or heirs or if your heirs do not claim Letters of Administration within 40 days after your death, Letters of Administration may be granted to anyone who applies and who is fit.

10. How Are Letters Of Administration Granted?

Any time after you die the person seeking to administer your estate appears at the Surrogate's office with the death certificate.

Your spouse is the first person entitled to administration. No consent to or renunciation of the right to administer your estate need be obtained from your heirs or next of kin.

If the person seeking to administer your estate is not your spouse, then he or she must have obtained consents or renunciations from or given written notice to the other heirs or next of kin who may also have the right to administer your estate.

The person making application signs a legal document, known as a complaint, which recites his or her residence, your name and date of death, the address you lived at when you died, the names and addresses of your spouse, heirs, next of kin, and other persons who may be entitled to letters of administration and their relationships, the ages of any minor heirs or next of kin.

Then he or she files the death certificate and an affidavit as to the value of your estate.

If you die without a will, the Surrogate will require that the person seeking to be appointed Administrator post a bond for faithful performance of his or her duties in an amount to be set by the Surrogate (usually the value of your estate).

Note: A bond is no longer required for a surviving spouse who inherits the entire estate.

Then the Surrogate grants the Letters of Administration.

Note: This discussion has not included certain other procedures at the Surrogate's office. Also, Letters of Administration will not be granted, and instead a court hearing will be held, if any of the interested persons receiving notice of the application object to the appointment sought.

---

11. How Much Does All This Cost?

The initial visit to the Surrogate usually runs under $200.00. The Appendix lists some other fees.

The **cost of the bond**, the annual premium, is another matter. Random quotes have produced the following:

Amount	Premium
$ 20,000.00	$ 110.00
50,000.00	260.00
100,000.00	560.00
200,000.00	860.00
300,000.00	1,110.00
400,000.00	1,360.00
500,000.00	1,610.00
1,500,000.00	3,760.00

12. Then What Does The Administrator Do? What Are The Duties And The Powers?

The *legal duty* imposed on the Administrator is to settle and distribute the estate in accordance with the law and, to quote the statutory language, "as expeditiously and efficiently as is consistent with the best interests of the estate."

The Administrator has to deal with the estate assets as would "a prudent man dealing with the property of another." Moreover, if the Administrator has special skills, he or she has a duty to use them.

If the Administrator has questions concerning the estate or its administration, he or she can, on written notice to all interested parties, apply to the court for instructions as to what to do.

Toward these ends the Administrator has the right and duty, with certain practical exceptions, to take possession of your property.

The powers conferred on the Administrator by law are extensive and complex. By way of brief summary, they include the powers: to accept additions to the estate, to invest and reinvest the assets, to keep insurance policies in force, to possess, manage and sell real and personal property, to employ and compensate attorneys, to settle claims for or against the estate, to enter into contracts, continue your business, to join with your spouse in filing joint income tax returns.

At this point the duties and powers and liabilities of the Administrator will be continued later under the discussion dealing with Personal Representatives because the Administration of your estate had you died without a will for the most part is the same as the administration of your estate had you died with a will.

PART II:
DYING WITH A WILL

1. What Is A Will And How Is It Made?

A will is a written document specifying how you want your property to be disposed of after your death.

If you are 18 years old or older and of sound mind, you can make a will.

In order for a will to be valid it must meet certain requirements. It has to be: (a) In writing and (b) signed by you and (c) also signed by at least two persons who each either witnessed your signing of the will or witnessed your acknowledgment that the signature on the will is yours.

Your will can also be made ***self-proved*** by meeting certain other requirements in the presence of a notary public or New Jersey attorney for the purpose of simplifying the admission of your will to probate at the Surrogate's office after your death. This will be explained later at page 23.

There is one exception to the above requirements: New Jersey law permits a ***holographic will***, which is a written will, the material provisions of which are in your handwriting and signed by you at the end.

2. What Does Sound Mind Mean? (And Other Requirements)

Generally, **sound mind** means that you must have the mental capacity to comprehend that you own property, that you know how much and what kind of property you have, that you know the persons to whom you wish to leave your property, and that the document you are signing (your will) is the document that will leave the property to whom you want upon your death. In brief, you cannot be insane or feebleminded.

Moreover, there are some other requirements:

You cannot make a mistake. In other words, you cannot, for your will to be valid, sign a will when you think you are signing a letter or something else.

Nor is your will valid if it is the result of fraud or undue influence. One example of the undue influence might be where a stranger, knowing you are old and frail, exploits this condition and persuades you to leave everything to him instead of your children.

These problems of **sound mind**, **mistake**, **fraud** and **undue influence** are dealt with after your death at a court hearing.

3. Can You Will Your Property To Whomever You Want? (And The Right Of Election Of The Surviving Spouse)

Yes, with one exception: You cannot disinherit your spouse, because he or she has the right to choose to take a certain portion of your estate within a certain amount of time after your death no matter how you write your will.

Your spouse's share is:

An amount equal to one-third of your **augmented estate**.

This right is available only if at the time of your death you and your spouse had been living together as man and wife. If at the time of your death you and your spouse had been living separate and apart and in different places or had ceased to live together as man and wife, the right of election is not available.

Your **augmented estate** is arrived at using a complex calculation. First, calculate the gross value of your estate. Then subtract funeral and administration expenses and the value of enforceable claims. Then add the value of certain kinds of transfers made before you died (but do not include such items as life insurance or pensions). The result is your **augmented estate** (usually a lengthy, difficult calculation).

Your spouse can surrender this right of election under some circumstances. Many times, when two spouses marry for the second time, and each spouse has children from a previous marriage, and each spouse wants to preserve his or her respective assets for each spouse's children, then they may sign what is known as an ante nuptial or pre marital agreement, and in this agreement each spouse may give up the right to take against the other spouse's will.

Dower and Curtesy. This is the right of a surviving spouse for life to one-half of a decedent's real property. **Dower** is the right of the surviving wife. **Curtesy** is the right of the surviving husband. The right is valid only if the marriage was made **and** the real property acquired before May 28, 1980.

4. Can You Change Or Revoke Your Will?

Yes. At any time up until you die you can change, alter or amend or revoke your will. You can change, alter or amend your will by making a new will or a codicil and signing it and having it witnessed in the same way as you did your original will. (A **codicil**, by the way, is a document shorter than a will, signed and witnessed like a will, which explains or changes one or more provisions in a will).

You can revoke your will entirely by making a new will that revokes the former will or by physically destroying the will with the intent of revoking it.

Note: No bequest under a will or any clause of a will may be altered or changed except by the proper making of another will or codicil declaring such change or alteration in accordance with the requirements for making a will. **Therefore**: Don't change your will by writing on it and then initialing the changes.

---

5. What Are Some Of The Things You Can Put In Your Will?

You can do such things as the following:

1. You can determine which persons or institutions shall or shall not receive all or part of your estate.

2. You can determine which person or persons or institution or institutions, such as a bank, shall administer your estate as well as whether or not a bond shall be posted.

3. You can determine the form of any bequest you make under your will. For example, You may decide to leave money to a beneficiary outright or in trust. Trusts will be discussed later.

4. In some instances you can specify how you want some or all of your debts paid.

5. Depending on how you set your will up, you may be able to minimize state inheritance taxes and/or federal estate taxes.

The above list is not all-inclusive. And remember, as will be mentioned later, the will is only one estate planning tool.

6. *Some Common Questions About Wills*

1. What if you move to New Jersey and bring with you a will you made in another state and then die in New Jersey? Is the will you brought with you valid?

    A written will is considered to be validly made if (1) it is made in accordance with the requirements of New Jersey law or (2) it is made in compliance with the law of the state where it was originally made.

2. Can a person who is a beneficiary under your will be a witness to your will?

    Yes, *but:* The old law was the opposite, namely, that if a beneficiary witnessed a will the will was void as to that beneficiary. However, except for emergency circumstances, it would be bad practice to permit a beneficiary to witness a will because it could open the door to such issues as fraud or undue influence and the like.

3. Can a will refer to another writing which specifies how you want your property disposed of?

    Yes, and here's an example: You leave to your nephew, John, all that property you own specified on a certain list sealed in an envelope in your office safe.

4. Does New Jersey law always govern your estate and its administration?

   Yes, unless you state in your will — and you have the right to do this — which state law shall govern.

5. What if you make a will, then acquire property, then die? Does your will transfer this after-acquired property?

   Yes.

6. What if you make a will, then marry, but fail to change your will to provide for your new spouse?

   Your spouse receives the same share he or she would have received had you made no will (unless it appears from your will you intentionally meant to omit your spouse or you made other provisions for your spouse by way of transfer of property outside your will, such as by joint bank account, joint real estate, life insurance, and you intended such transfer to be in place of any provision under your will. All subject, however, to the spouse's right of election as previously discussed).

7. What if you make a will, then have or adopt children who are not provided for under the will?

   The omitted child or children receive the same share he or she or they would have received had you died without a will (unless it appears from your will you intentionally meant to omit your child or children *or* when you made your will you had a child or children and left substantially all of your estate to the other parent of the surviving child or children or you made other provisions for your child or children by way of transfer of property outside your will, such as by joint bank account, joint real estate, life insurance).

8. What if you make a will leaving everything to your spouse and then get divorced?

   Your will is automatically revoked. However, if you remarry that same person from whom you were divorced, your will is automatically revived.

9. If you make a will and then revoke it by making another will and then destroy the second will, is the first will revived?

   No. The first will is only revived by doing it all over again or by re-executing it or by making a codicil expressing your intent to revive it.

10. What if one of the beneficiaries under your will criminally and intentionally kills you?

    Such person loses the right to take under your will. The same law applies to the other joint tenant of your personal or real property as well as your beneficiary under your bond or life insurance policy.

11. What if someone intentionally conceals or destroys your will?

    In New Jersey that person would be guilty of a crime of the third degree.

12. Can you make your own will without going to a lawyer?

    Yes, but you should not and this will be discussed later.

Note: These are only a few of the many questions pertaining to wills.

---

7. Administration When You Die With A Will

This is repetition: Administration is the legal procedure which takes place from the time of your death until your estate is finally distributed to the person or persons entitled to it.

Administration takes place in the county in which you died a resident. The court which has jurisdiction is usually the Surrogate's Court, although the Superior Court, Probate Part, also has jurisdiction.

When you die with a will, the person who administers your estate, and who is usually named in your will (for the sake of simplicity this will be assumed) is called the **Executor**. When you die with a will you die testate. Your Executor, when appointed by the Surrogate, does the same thing with a **testate** estate that an Administrator does with an **intestate** estate:

1. Collects and preserves your assets (if required, invests or sells or even abandons them).

2. Pays your debts and your taxes.

3. Finds your beneficiaries and distributes your estate to them.

8. Is Administration Always Required?

No. There is no law which affirmatively requires that a will be probated. Nevertheless, for legal or practical reasons it would appear that whenever there is a will and some assets in your name, there is going to be probate and administration, no matter how minimal - even if only to endorse or negotiate some checks in your name alone.

Moreover, the law provides that in order for a will to be effective to prove the transfer of any property, such will must be admitted to probate. This is not necessarily saying that if you leave your farm to your friend Jack that Jack will not get the farm unless the will is probated and becomes a matter of public record. But it will certainly make matters much easier if your will is probated.

As has been stated previously, it is a crime to **intentionally conceal** a will. The obvious underlying theory concerns the alteration of property rights. If your son is your only heir and would take your entire estate in the event of your death without a will, and your will leaves your farm to your friend Jack, and your son conceals your will, your son has committed a crime.

Probate might not be necessary if you lived all alone and had no assets or if you were married with no children and all your assets were owned jointly with your spouse. However, for small nagging matters which may arise - such as the checks in your name or the car in your name - there will probably have to be some form of administration.

Question: If the assets are under $20,000 with a surviving spouse or under $10,000 with surviving children won't the previously discussed Affidavit In Lieu of Administration suffice? No. That's only available if you die without a will. The affidavit to be signed recites you died without a will.

Note: In those instances in which the assets are small the probate of a will and the administration of your estate is not, as some popular writers might state or imply, an expensive, lengthy process. At least it not need be.

---

9. What Are Letters Testamentary And To Whom Are They Granted?

Letters Testamentary are to the Executor of a testate estate as **Letters of Administration** are to the Administrator of an intestate estate.

Letters Testamentary are legal documents issued by the Surrogate to the Executor of your estate. They authorize and empower the Executor to administer your estate. Certified copies of Letters Testamentary are used along with other documents to do such things as open estate bank accounts and transfer estate assets.

Letters Testamentary are issued to the Executor named in your will (If your will names no Executor or if it does but he or she predeceases you, there is another procedure to be followed but it will not be discussed here).

However, the person seeking to be appointed Executor and issued Letters Testamentary must get your will admitted to probate.

10. What Is Probate And How Does It Take Place?

Probate is the procedure whereby your will is "proved" or established as the valid document which transfers your property at death.

As in the case of the appointment of an Administrator for an intestate estate, the person seeking to prove your will and get appointed as Executor of your estate appears with the death certificate and your will at the Surrogate's office of the County in which you died a resident. He or she signs a document known as a **complaint**, which recites his or her residence, your name, date of death, residence at date of death and date of the will, the names and addresses of your spouse, heirs, next of kin and other interested persons, the ages of any minor heirs or next of kin and whether you had lineal descendants living when the will was made, whether any children of yours were born after your will was made, whether there are any adopted children and their names and addresses.

At the same time, the will is offered for probate. There are two ways in which a will may be admitted to probate - *in common form* and *in solemn form*.

11. *Probate In Common And Solemn Form And The Will Contest*

If a will is *self-proved* - which was discussed previously and which required your signature as well as the signature of two witnesses in a special form in the presence of a notary public or a New Jersey attorney - then the will is automatically admitted to probate without further proof. (Assuming, of course, that on its face and by all appearances the will is proper - no erasures or alterations or obviously misnamed beneficiaries.)

If the will is not self-proved but is otherwise validly executed, at least one of the witnesses must sign an affidavit concerning your proper making of the will. If both witnesses are deceased, their signatures may be proved by another person. Then, if the will appears to be in order (see above paragraph) it is admitted to probate.

Most wills are admitted to probate this way, *in common form*.

Probate *in solemn form* is done on notice to all interested parties at a full court hearing before a judge. Probate in solemn form would be required if there was an apparent defect on the face of the will, such as an alteration or misnamed beneficiary.

Probate in solemn form is also required if there is a holographic will.

If an interested person challenges the validity of your will, on such grounds as fraud, mistake, or undue influence, a full court hearing is required. The challenge which precipitates the court hearing can be made before or after the will is admitted to probate within certain time limitations.

Although probate proceedings may begin at any time after your death, your will cannot be admitted to probate until at least ten days after your death.

> Note: After a will is admitted to probate in common form, the Executor must notify all interested parties of this within 60 days. One of the reasons for this is to give them the opportunity to challenge the will if they so desire.

12. How Much Does All This Cost?

As stated previously, New Jersey law sets forth a schedule of fees. The cost for probating the will and obtaining Letters Testamentary, assuming there is no challenge or other complication, is approximately the same as that for obtaining Letters of Administration. Some of the fees are set forth in the Appendix but for the sake of the present discussion, the initial visit to the Surrogate usually runs under $200.00.

The cost of the bond, as has been stated, is another matter; and when the will by its terms appoints a named resident Executor, no bond is required to be posted. In fact, as a matter of course, wills which name Executors usually direct they serve without bond. The will may, of course, appoint an Executor and direct he or she post a bond. (See page __ for a schedule of bond premiums).

13. Then What Does The Executor Do? What are The Duties And Powers?

Essentially, unless the will by its terms specifies otherwise, the Executor of the testate estate has the same duties and powers as the Administrator of the intestate estate (see previous discussion):

To settle and distribute the estate in accordance with the law as expeditiously and efficiently as is consistent with the best interests of the estate.

To deal with the estate assets as would a prudent man dealing with the property of another and to use whatever special skills he may have.

If the Executor has questions concerning the estate or its administration, he or she can, on notice to all interested parties, apply to the court for instructions as to what to do.

Toward these ends, the Executor has the right and duty, with certain practical exceptions, to take possession of your property.

The powers conferred on the Executor by law are extensive and complex. By way of brief summary, they include the power (unless limited or expanded by the terms of the will): To accept additions to the estate, to invest and reinvest the assets, to keep insurance policies in force, to possess, manage and sell real and personal property, to employ and compensate attorneys, to settle claims for or against the estate, to enter into contracts, continue your business, to join with your spouse in filing joint income tax returns.

14. Notice Of Probate Of The Will

To repeat: Within 60 days after the probate of the will, the Executor is required to mail a notice to all beneficiaries and next of kin of the date and place of probate, as well as a statement that a copy of the will shall be furnished upon request. The Executor is then required to file a proof of mailing of this notice with the Surrogate's Court.

PART III:
ADMINISTERING THE ESTATE

1. Administering The Estate After Letters Of Administration Or Letters Testamentary Are Granted

For the most part, the duties of the Administrator of the intestate estate and the duties of the Executor of the testate estate are similar. Hence, in the following discussion both will be referred to as the *Personal Representative*.

The Personal Representative is a person with a distinct legal entity, as is the estate for which he or she is responsible. It has been said that for all intents and purposes, the Personal Representative stands in your shoes and carries out the necessary duties and exercises the necessary powers until your estate is distributed, at which time, with the following of certain procedures, the role of the Personal Representative ends.

The Personal Representative has the capacity to sue on behalf of your estate and to be sued on behalf of your estate; and if the Personal Representative commits a wrongful act, he or she can be sued individually.

Until the appointment is terminated, the Personal Representative has the same power over the title to property that an absolute owner would have, in trust however, for the benefit of the creditors and others interested in the estate. The trust relationship also makes the Personal Representative a *Fiduciary*. A Fiduciary is a person who holds a special trust relationship and includes not only Personal Representatives but, as seen later, Trustees and Guardians as well.

2. *Some Procedural Steps*

1. ***Notifying the Social Security Administration***. If you were receiving monthly Social Security checks at the time of your death, they should stop. It is a crime to collect Social Security benefits on a deceased person. Moreover, your estate or next of kin may be entitled to other benefits. One benefit is the credit toward the funeral expense.

2. ***Notifying the Veterans Administration***. If you were a veteran your estate or next of kin may be entitled to benefits.

3. ***Opening an Estate Account***. This simple procedure is usually required in the smallest estates because there is at least one check, probably a paycheck, in your name which has to be properly endorsed by your Personal Representative. The cost of opening an estate account is usually no more than opening a regular checking account. It is in the name of the estate. Into it are deposited not only checks in your name but the proceeds of the sale of your estate assets.

4. ***Opening a Safe Deposit Box***. If there are tangible or intangible valuables, such as the gold watch or the diamond ring or the stock certificate, they should be safely preserved. The cost of a safe deposit box is relatively small and is an expense of administration.

5. ***Opening your safe deposit box***. There is much mystery surrounding safe deposit boxes in the name of a decedent alone or in the joint names of decedent and another. The box is not automatically ***sealed*** upon death. At the very least access is permitted in order to get the will and any deeds.

6. ***Obtaining your tax returns.*** Your Personal Representative should obtain copies of your income tax returns for the past three years. The New Jersey Transfer Inheritance Tax Branch, and sometimes the Internal Revenue Service, may require this information.

Sometimes the Personal Representative has difficulty locating all your property. Your affairs may be in miserable condition or certain persons who know about your property may be uncooperative.

The Personal Representative can hire the proper experts, such as investigators, to locate any of your property. And the Personal Representative may go to court and obtain a court order for the purposes of investigation, the taking of testimony from any person who may have knowledge as to the extent and value of your property, together with the power to subpoena books, papers, and any other documents which bear on this issue.

3. Claims Against The Estate

The persons or parties who have claims against your estate are the ***creditors***. The Personal Representative is obliged to seek out the creditors and pay them with estate assets.

Creditors shall present their claims to the Personal Representative in writing and under oath within 9 months from the date of death.

If the estate has insufficient assets, the Personal Representative may have the court declare the estate to be ***insolvent*** and pay the creditors with whatever assets there are in the following order:

1. Reasonable funeral expenses.

2. Costs and expenses of administration.

3. Debts and taxes.

4. Reasonable medical and hospital expenses of your last illness.

5. Judgments entered against you.

6. All other claims.

Note: As was previously stated, there are situations where administration is not always required. (See page 8.)

The following discussion includes some claims against the estate (but not necessarily in the above order listed).

4. Medical Expenses

If there was a last illness, your estate will be responsible for the payment of your hospital and medical expenses.

The responsibilities of the Personal Representative include collecting all the hospital and medical bills, submitting them to the proper insurance company for payment - whether Blue Cross, Blue Shield or a private insurance company - and if there are balances remaining which are not covered by insurance, then finding the necessary funds from the estate to pay them.

5. Funeral Expenses

Funeral expenses are first on the list of claims to be paid.

Your funeral almost always occurs before the will is admitted to probate. So when your next of kin appear at the funeral home the funeral director may insist one of them personally sign the contract for the funeral arrangements. In so doing, the funeral director can get double protection. A claim for funeral charges can be brought against your estate or against the person who independently signed for the funeral.

The law provides that an Executor may carry out your written instructions pertaining to your body, funeral and burial arrangements **before** appointment. Often the Social Security Administration provides a credit for funeral expenses and the Veterans Administration in certain instances has an allowance for burial markers. And any person who pays part or all of the funeral expenses has a right to reimbursement from the estate.

6. *The New Jersey Transfer Inheritance Tax*

It is a *tax on the transfer or passing of your property to another person by reason of your death*.

It is paid by the person who receives the property (unless your will directs otherwise).

It is determined as follows:

1. The gross value of your estate is calculated.

2. From that gross value there are subtracted certain deductions.

3. The net value of each share passing to each beneficiary is then ascertained.

4. The tax is then calculated and paid. The Transfer Inheritance Tax is due within eight months of your death. If it is not paid at that time, then interest on the unpaid balance accumulates at ten percent per year until the tax is paid.

The Personal Representative is required to file a Transfer Inheritance Tax Return within eight months of your death. It may be necessary to file it, even if there is no tax due, in order to obtain the *release of tax liens* which automatically attach to much of your real and personal property. In other words, many of your estate assets cannot be transferred unless the Inheritance Tax Branch is paid the tax or receives evidence that no tax is due or is given the proper request for a ***tax waiver.*** A ***tax waiver*** is the formal consent from the Branch to release the tax lien and transfer the estate asset in question.

Note: The Branch will now issue tax waivers on certain assets upon the filing of a special affidavit instead of a full return where there is no taxable estate and the value of the estate does not exceed $675,000.00. The New Jersey Estate tax is discussed at Page 44.

---

7. What Items Are Includible In The Gross Value Of Your Estate?

The following list, though not all-inclusive, will give a general idea.

1. ***Real property*** located in New Jersey in which you have an interest - a sole interest, a part interest, or a joint interest with right of survivorship (except real property owned jointly by you and your spouse).

2. ***Tangible personal property*** located in New Jersey in which you have an interest - a sole interest, a part interest, or a joint interest with right of survivorship. Tangible personal property is physical personal property such as motor vehicles, furniture, boats, etc.

3. ***Intangible personal property*** located in New Jersey or outside New Jersey in which you have an interest - a sole interest, a part interest, or a joint interest with right of survivorship. Intangible personal property includes such things as stocks, bonds, mortgages and the like. It would also include the value of your business or partnership interest as well as the value of claims you

may have against others such as debts due you from others or life insurance payable to your estate.

4. ***Real or personal property which you have transferred to another within three years of your death for inadequate consideration*** (little or no money; in other words, a gift), unless your Personal Representative can prove the transfer was ***not made in contemplation of your own death*** in order to avoid inheritance taxes.

   For exampe: You are on your death bed and sign a withdrawal slip for the bank account in your name alone and it is transferred to your son before you die. It is perfectly legal to do this. However, the value of your bank account is includible in your estate for inheritance tax purposes and must be so reported.

Note: You are deemed also to be the ***full owner*** of all jointly owned property unless your Personal Representative or the survivor can prove the contrary - namely, that your survivor furnished or paid for all or a part of the property. (This does not include real property owned jointly by you and your spouse with right of survivorship.)

---

8. What Items Are Generally <u>Not</u> Includible In The Gross Value Of Your Estate?

1. ***Real property*** held by you and your spouse in joint ownership with the right of survivorship (this is known as a ***tenancy by the entirety***). The most common example is the home you and your spouse own. The law has been amended to include a cooperative apartment owned by you and your spouse.

> Note: This exemption is probably obsolete for decedents dying after January 1, 1985 as after that date there is no tax on property passing to a surviving spouse.

2. **Life insurance proceeds** payable to a named beneficiary other than your estate.

3. **Property passing to the State of New Jersey** or any of its political subdivisions or to a New Jersey municipality for an "exclusive public use or purpose" or to a **public** or **charitable** or **religious** or **educational** institution.

4. Many types of **government** and **private pension** or **retirement proceeds** pursuant to certain federal or state laws.

> Note: If there is a personal injury claim, part of the proceeds from it may be includible and part of it may be excludable from your gross estate.

9. What is Deductible From The Gross Value Of Your Estate?

1. Your **debts**.

2. Your reasonable **funeral expenses** and the expenses of your **last illness**.

3. The **costs** and **expenses** of the **administration** of your estate, including the commissions of your Personal Representative and the fees of your attorney.

4. A certain proportion of state, county and local **taxes** imposed upon your property.

5. Transfer **taxes** paid to other states by virtue of your death (but not the Federal Estate Tax).

10. What Are The New Jersey Inheritance Tax Rates?

It depends on which class your beneficiary belongs:

1. For the transfer to your spouse, parent, grandparent, child or grandchild (Class A beneficiaries) there is no tax.

2. For the transfer to your brother, sister, son-in-law or daughter-in-law (Class C beneficiaries) there is no tax on amounts transferred up to $25,000.00.

   Then the rates are:

Amount of Transfer on any amount:	Tax
Up to 1,100,000	11%
Over 1,100,000 up to 1,400,000	13%
Over 1,400,000 up to 1,700,000	14%
Over 1,700,000	16%

To everyone else (Class D beneficiaries), every other transferee or beneficiary (except exempt beneficiaries as previously stated, such as a charity):

Amount of Transfer* On any amount:	Tax
Up to 700,000	15%
Over 700,000	16%

*There is no tax if the share is less than $500, but there is the *full tax* if the share exceeds $500.

To Summarize:

A. Calculate the value of the gross estate, which includes:

1. Real property in New Jersey.

2. Tangible personal property in New Jersey.

3. Intangible personal property wherever located.

4. Real or personal property you gave to another within three years of death.

Note: Include the total value of joint owned property with right of survivorship unless it can be proven the survivor paid for or furnished all or part of the consideration.

Note: The gross estate does not include:

1. Real property owned by you and your spouse jointly with right of survivorship.

2. Life insurance proceeds payable to a named beneficiary other than your estate.

3. Property passing to the State of New Jersey or to charity.

4. Many types of government and private pension or retirement proceeds.

B. Deduct the following from the gross estate:

1. Your debts.

2. Your funeral expenses.

3. The costs and expenses of administration.

4. Certain state, county and local taxes imposed on your property.

5. Transfer taxes paid to other states by virtue of your death.

C. Calculate the amount due each beneficiary and then calculate the tax.

11. The Federal Estate Tax

It is a tax on the value of your estate at the time of your death (or on the value of your estate at six months after your death if the Personal Representative so elects).

It is determined as follows:

1. The **gross value** of your estate is calculated.

2. **Certain deductions** are subtracted.

3. The **tentative tax** is calculated.

4. **Certain credits** are subtracted.

5. The **Federal Estate Tax** is the resulting balance.

The general rule is that the Personal Representative must file the return and pay the tax within nine months of your death. The failure to either pay the tax or file the return results in the imposition of interest and penalty charges. However, an automatic six month extension is available, but this does not stop the imposition of interest for payments made beyond the nine month period.

Also, in some cases, most notably where most of your estate consists of the stock in a closely-held or small business or family corporation, there will be exceptions to this general rule, such as permitting payments in installments.

Most **estates do not have to pay a federal estate tax** (though a federal estate tax return may have to be filed even if there is no tax due). You may be able to determine if your estate falls in this category under the heading Federal Estate Tax Exemption. (See page 43.)

12. What Items Are Includible In The Gross Value Of Your Estate?

All property in which you owned an interest at the time of your death. The following list, though not all-inclusive, should give e general idea.

1. Any ***real property***, wherever located, in which you have an interest, sole, part or joint.

> Note: Under New Jersey law real property owned jointly by husband and wife is exempt.

2. ***Tangible personal property*** (the bank accounts, the stocks,etc.), wherever located, in which you have an interest, sole, part or joint.

3. ***Intangible personal property***, wherever located, in which you have an interest, sole, part or joint.

4. The face value of the ***proceeds of life insurance***.

> Note: Under New Jersey law life insurance payable to a named beneficiary is excluded.

5. Within certain limits, some ***pension and retirement plan proceeds***.

> Note: Under New Jersey law these were generally excluded.

6. ***Property transferred during your lifetime in which you retained all or a portion of it***. Such property might include a gift which was revocable by you or in which you retained the right to enjoy the income of or which was only to take effect upon your death.

Note: Under New Jersey law gifts made within three years of death are includible in your gross estate unless your Personal Representative can prove the transfer was not made in contemplation of your own death in order to avoid inheritance taxes. Under federal law this used to be the rule but is no longer. You can make a gift at any time before your death so long as it is absolute and irrevocable with no retained interest. It could, however, be subject to the federal gift tax.

One final point on joint ownership: New Jersey law on joint ownership, namely: that you are presumed to own *all* of the property unless your Personal Representative or your survivor can prove otherwise, is also the federal law *with one exception*: In federal law husband and wife are treated as owning joint property one-half each. So, if you and your spouse own a house as joint tenants by the entirety with the right of survivorship when you die, then one-half the value of the house and not the entire value of the house will be included in your gross estate.

13. What Is Deductible From The Gross Value Of Your Estate?

1. Your *debts*.

2. Your reasonable *funeral expenses* and expenses of your *last illness*.

3. The *costs* and *expenses* of the *administration* of your estate, including the commissions of your Personal Representative and the fees of your attorney.

4. Any and all *bequests or transfers to your surviving spouse* (this deduction is known as the *marital deduction*).

5. Transfers to *charitable* and other public institutions.

14. The Calculation Of The Federal Estate Tax

From your **gross estate** there is subtracted the sum of your **deductions**. The result is your **taxable estate**.

A **tentative tax** is then calculated on your taxable estate in accordance with the following schedule on the next page:

If the amount is:		Tentative Tax is:		
Over	But not over	Tax + %	On excess over	
$ 0	$ 10,000	$ 0	18%	$ 0
10,000	20,000	1,800	20	10,000
20,000	40,000	3,800	22	20,000
40,000	60,000	8,200	24	40,000
60,000	80,000	13,000	26	60,000
80,000	100,000	18,200	28	80,000
100,000	150,000	23,800	30	100,000
150,000	250,000	38,800	32	150,000
250,000	500,000	70,800	34	250,000
500,000	750,000	155,800	37	500,000
750,000	1,000,000	248,300	39	750,000
1,000,000	1,250,000	345,800	41	1,000,000
1,250,000	1,500,000	448,300	43	1,250,000
1,500,000	2,000,000	555,800	45	1,500,000
2,000,000	2,500,000	780,800	48	2,000,000
2,500,000	---	1,025,800	50	2,500,000

The phased-in rate changes are as follows:

	If the amount is:		Tentative Tax is:		
Year	Over	But not over	Tax + %	On excess over	
2005	$ 2,000,000	---	$ 780,800	47	$ 2,000,000
2006	2,000,000	---	780,800	46	2,000,000
2007-	1,250,000	$ 1,500,000	448,300	43	1,250,000
2009	1,500,000	---	555,800	45	1,500,000

In 2010 the tax is repealed, but in 2011 the tax is re-imposed as it was in effect on December 31, 2001. On December 31, 2001 the federal estate tax was levied on estates over $675,000.00

From the **tentative tax** there is subtracted the total of **federal gift taxes**, if any, paid in previous years for gifts made, in order to arrive at the gross estate tax.

From the **gross estate tax** there is subtracted (with a few technical adjustments) the **unified credit** and the **state tax death** credit.

The **unified credit** is $555,800.00 in 2005; $780,000.00 in 2006, 2007 and 2008; and $1,455,800 in 2009.

The **state tax death credit** is the actual amount of inheritance taxes paid New Jersey and/or any other state.

The result (again with a few technical adjustments, including New Jersey Inheritance taxes actually paid) is the federal estate tax due.

Note: The above description of the federal estate tax, as well as the New Jersey Transfer Inheritance Tax, is for the sole purpose of painting a very broad picture as to what is involved. There are numerous technicalities and subtleties under state and federal law which determine what is included or excluded or deducted in and from your estate. This description has omitted, for the sake of simplicity, several such items. Therefore, do not attempt to calculate the federal estate taxes from this book.

To Summarize:

A. Calculate the value of the gross estate, which includes:

1. Real property wherever located.

2. Personal property, tangible and intangible, wherever located.

3. Life insurance proceeds.

4. Within certain limits, pension and retirement plan proceeds.

5. Property transferred with a retained life interest.

> Note: Joint property with right of survivorship is fully includible unless the survivor can prove he or she furnished all or part of the consideration for it. **But** only half of the value of the property owned jointly by husband and wife with right of survivorship is includible.

B. Deduct the following from the gross estate:

1. Your debts.

2. Your funeral expenses.

3. The costs and expenses of administration, including court fees, Executor's commissions and professional fees (attorney and accountant).

4. Any and all bequests and transfers to your surviving spouse.

5. Transfers to charitable and other public institutions.

C. Calculate the tentative tax.

D. From the tentative tax subtract any gift taxes paid in previous years.

E. From this result, subtract the unified credit and the actual amount of inheritance taxes paid New Jersey and/or other state(s).

F The result is the federal estate tax due.

15. The Federal Estate Tax Exemption

Your estate may ***not*** have to pay federal estate taxes. If you leave everything to your spouse, and he/she is a U.S. citizen, there is ***no*** federal estate tax due. This is because of the unlimited marital deduction. Moreover, whether you are married or single, there is no federal estate tax due in the following years if your estate does not exceed the following amounts:

YEARS	AMOUNTS
2005	1,500,000.00
2006, 2007 and 2008	2,000.000.00
2009	3,500,000.00
2010	No tax

After 2010 the tax rates in effect as of December 31, 2001 take effect unless Congress does something. The exemption amount on December 31, 2001 was $675,000.00.

Note: Even if there is no federal estate tax due, your Personal Representative may still have to file a federal estate tax return within nine months from the date of your death if the value of your ***gross estate*** was at least the credit exemption amount in the year you died.

16. The New Jersey Estate Tax

This is <u>not</u> the New Jersey Transfer Inheritance Tax.

Even if your estate is not subject federal estate taxes, it may nevertheless be subject to New Jersey Estate taxes because of a new statute enacted in July 2002 and made retroactive to January 1, 2002.

The New Jersey Estate tax is calculated on your estate as if you had died on December 31, 2001. On December 31, 2001 the federal estate tax exemption was $675,000.00.

Consider the following example:

You die in 2005 with a net estate worth $1,000,000.00. Since the value of your estate is less than the $1,500,000.00 federal estate tax exemption, no federal estate tax is due.

If your only beneficiaries are your spouse and/or children, there is no New Jersey Inheritance tax due.

However, there is a New Jersey Estate tax due, because your estate exceeds the $675,000.00 federal exemption amount in effect on December 31, 2001.

The New Jersey Estate tax is calculated as follows:

Start with the gross estate amount and subtract the estate expenses as if a federal estate tax form was being completed. In this example the net estate amount is $1,000,000.00. From this $1,000,000.00 subtract the sum of $60,000.00 and you get $940,000.00, which is the <u>adjusted</u> <u>taxable</u> <u>estate</u>.

Then go to the following table:

Adjusted Taxable Estate From	To	Credit = Amount +	%	Of Excess Over
$ 0	$ 40,000	$ 0	0	$ 0
40,000	90,000	0	.8	40,000
90,000	140,000	400	1.6	90,000
140,000	240,000	1,200	2.4	140,000
240,000	440,000	3,600	3.2	240,000
440,000	640,000	10,000	4.0	440,000
640,000	840,000	18,000	4.8	640,000
840,000	1,040,000	27,600	5.6	840,000
1,040,000	1,540,000	38,800	6.4	1,040,000
1,540,000	2,040,000	70,800	7.2	1,540,000
2,040,000	2,540,000	106,800	8.0	2,040,000
2,540,000	3,040,000	146,800	8.8	2,540,000
3,040,000	3,540,000	190,800	9.6	3,040,000
3,540,000	4,040,000	238,800	10.4	3,540,000
4,040,000	5,040,000	290,800	11.2	4,040,000
5,040,000	6,040,000	402,800	12.0	5,040,000
6,040,000	7,040,000	522,800	12.8	6,040,000
7,040,000	8,040,000	650,800	13.6	7,040,000
8,040,000	9,040,000	786,800	14.4	8,040,000
9,040,000	10,040,000	930,800	15.2	9,040,000
10,040,000	-----	1,082,800	16.0	10,040,000

17. Other Expenses of Administration

Costs and expenses of administration include but are not necessarily limited to such things as the following:

1. Funeral and burial expenses.

2. Fees for attorneys, accountants and appraisers.

3. Court costs.

4. Commissions for the Personal Representative.

5. Debts, including funeral and medical expenses.

The costs and expenses of administration are incurred from the beginning of the estate, when the Personal Representative is appointed until the final winding up of the estate. These costs and expenses may have priority over other creditors, as can be seen from the list previously presented under Claims Against the Estate.

Some of these items will be developed in more detail in subsequent headings.

18. Claims Of The Estate

Claims are **assets** of your estate.

It may or may not take some investigation on the part of your Personal Representative to discover who your debtors are. The course of action to follow is obvious. The Personal Representative makes inquiries from the proper sources. If a recoverable claim is discovered, it is pursued against the proper parties. If a lawsuit is required, the Personal Representative has the power to sue.

The real issue as to claims of the estate may be less than obvious. One example:

The **circumstances of your death**. If your death arose out of and in the course of your employment, then your Personal Representative and/or your immediate next of kin may be able to make a claim for **worker's compensation benefits**.

In addition, or in the alternative, there may exist grounds for bringing other personal injury claims such as claims for medical malpractice or exposure to asbestos, etc. Perhaps the most obvious example would be if you were killed in a motor vehicle accident.

In any event, the Personal Representative has the responsibility to make the proper investigation and to consult with an attorney who knows this area of the law in order to discover the nature and extent of any claims.

19. Bank Accounts

In your name alone. The Personal Representative should close out your bank accounts and deposit the proceeds in the estate account. One half the proceeds may be withdrawn. To withdraw the other half a tax waiver is required from the New Jersey Transfer Inheritance Branch.

(As previously stated, a *tax waiver* is a document by which the New Jersey Transfer Inheritance Branch consents to the transfer of estate property which is subject to its lien for payment of taxes. In order to obtain a tax waiver an Inheritance Tax Return or facts giving reasonable assurance that the account can be released without jeopardizing the collection of the taxes, is filed with the Branch.)

In your name and another's jointly with right of survivorship. These funds are not subject to administration; they belong to the survivor subject, however, to a claim by the Transfer Inheritance Tax Branch. The survivor may withdraw half the funds. To release the other half a tax waiver is required.

In your name as trustee for another. During your lifetime you may deposit or withdraw at will, but at your death, the account belongs to the beneficiary and is not subject to administration. The tax waiver is required for the funds to be paid to the beneficiary, but if the beneficiary is under the age of eighteen, special **guardianship rules**, as discussed later, may apply. Half the proceeds may still be withdrawn.

Note: Because of the transfer inheritance tax amendments, tax waivers for certain beneficiaries are not required. A form affidavit will be sufficient.

---

20. Life Insurance

Usually the proceeds of life insurance are payable upon death to the surviving beneficiary; and the items to be submitted to the insurance company consist of the death certificate, the insurance policy itself, and a completed claim form supplied by the insurance company.

Life insurance policy proceeds are almost always payable to the named beneficiary or beneficiaries. So before distribution, the alternative options should be explored, especially if the beneficiary is the surviving spouse, other than a lump sum payment.

21. The Automobile

If you owned a **motor vehicle**, your Personal Representative should immediately contact your liability insurance company (or agent or broker) to confirm that the proper automobile insurance has been issued, is in effect, and is paid up to date.

Usually, by the terms of the policy, your spouse or a member of your household who lived with you or your Personal Representative can drive the car, but this should be reconfirmed with the automobile insurance company (or agent or broker).

The motor vehicle is an asset to be maintained by the Personal Representative. Driving it extensively during the course of administration depreciates this asset, so as a practical matter it may be best to keep it under lock and key, transfer it to the proper beneficiary or sell it to a third person and deposit the proceeds in the estate account.

The transfer of the automobile can usually be accomplished by presenting to the local Motor Vehicle Agency the Certificate of Title duly endorsed by the Personal Representative together with a copy of the Letters of Administration or Letters Testamentary. No tax waiver from the New Jersey Transfer Inheritance Tax Branch is necessary.

The automobile is an asset of the estate and has to be valued. Ordinarily an appraiser does not have to be retained. The values of most makes of automobiles are usually available in standard books kept by the automobile dealer or the insurance broker. These values are also available on the internet at Kelley's Blue Book website: www.kbb.com.

22. Real Estate

If real property does not pass to another on your death by right of survivorship, the Personal Representative should see it is properly **maintained and preserved** until it is distributed or sold or otherwise disposed of as your will directs.

Unless limited by the terms of your will, the Personal Representative has the **power to sell** real property. Should this be done during the course of administration? The answer depends on various factors: (1) the nature of the real property (a house, a farm, an apartment building); (2) the age and circumstances of the beneficiary or beneficiaries (an elderly widow or a son living in California); (3) the condition of the real property; (4) the amount of assets and debts of your estate; (5) and of course several other factors which will probably arise in each particular case.

If you and your spouse owned real property jointly with right of survivorship (as tenants *by the entirety*), upon your death your spouse automatically becomes the owner without need for administration or probate. As previously stated, such property is *exempt* from the New Jersey Inheritance Transfer Tax and, if subject to the federal estate tax, one half of it is included in your gross estate.

If you and another (not your spouse) owned real property jointly with right of survivorship (as *joint tenants*), upon your death the survivor automatically becomes the owner without need for administration or probate. For tax purposes you will be charged with full ownership unless it can be proved your survivor purchased all or part of it.

If you owned the real property alone or with others *without a right of survivorship* (*tenancy in common*), then the real property is an administration or probate asset and is includible in your gross estate for New Jersey and federal inheritance and estate tax purposes.

Except for the tenancy by the entirety (the husband and wife joint ownership) there will have to be a valuation of your real property interest by an expert appraiser.

Except for the tenancy by the entirety, before real property is sold a tax waiver will have to be obtained from the New Jersey Transfer Inheritance Tax Branch. Also, and this includes the tenancy by the entirety, in some cases a *release of lien* will have to be obtained from the *Internal Revenue Service*. There are special procedures for obtaining both.

Note: New Jersey law provides that your *real property is liable for payment of all your debts for one year after your death*. If your Personal Representative wants to sell your real property within one year of your death, he will have to obtain a proper court order which makes appropriate protec-

---

tive provisions for creditors. As a practical matter usually the purchaser of real property will agree to take title to it without requiring the court order if the Personal Representative swears in an affidavit at the time of sale that all your debts have been paid or provided for.

23. Pension Plans And Retirement Accounts

These include the accumulated proceeds of corporate pension and/or profit sharing plans as well as the individual self-employed retirement accounts - the "Keoghs", the 401(k)'s and the "IRA's".

Usually, as in life insurance, there is a named beneficiary, or these proceeds may be payable to the estate. In any event, these funds have to be released and distributed to the persons or parties entitled to them (including the Personal Representative if that is the case). The procedure involves contacting that institution which has the funds - a **bank** or **insurance** company or **your employer**. These institutions usually have personnel who can explain the requirements for transfer. Some of the items needed include the death certificate, a copy of Letters of Administration or Letters Testamentary, a tax waiver (or if the institution is outside New Jersey, no tax waiver but an affidavit to the effect that you died a resident of New Jersey).

The value of these funds may or may not be taxable under the New Jersey or federal law. Hence two considerations:

1. There will have to be a **valuation** of these funds as of the time of your death, and the institution which holds these funds will usually give such valuation on request. Moreover, in some cases these funds are a combination of what you and your employer each contributed over a number of years. Valuation for tax purposes is therefore not always that obvious or simple; yet, to repeat, the

institution involved, upon request, can usually do the work to meet the necessary requirements and provide the proper valuation.

2. There may not only be estate but also income tax exposure with respect to these funds. Therefore, as with life insurance, the beneficiary or the Personal Representative should give consideration as to what alternative distribution method may be available other than by way of a lump sum pay-out.

Note: If an alternative distribution is contemplated, there may be legal time limits within which a choice can be made. The beneficiary or the Personal Representative should act promptly.

---

24. Stocks And Bonds (Listed)

The Personal Representative will become involved in taking possession of stocks and bonds and other such securities, having them properly valued, and then holding them in their original form, selling them or distributing them to the interested beneficiaries.

Taking possession: The securities are usually at your home, in a safe deposit box, or in the "street name" at your brokerage house. If not in street name, they should be placed in the Personal Representative's safe deposit box. If in street name at the brokerage house, they can be left there or put into your Personal Representative's name.

Transferring them: To be transferred to the Personal Representative's name or the beneficiary's name, or to be sold or otherwise transferred, the requirements of the institution rendering the service - the bank or brokerage house - will have to be followed. Usually the requirements consist of the Personal Representative signing the security (or the equivalent stock power) with the signature guaranteed (a special procedure different from notarization), and delivering the security together with a copy of the Letters of Administration or Letters Testamentary. If the company which issued the security was organized in New Jersey, then a tax waiver from the New Jersey Transfer Inheritance Tax Branch may have to be obtained. In certain circumstances a release of lien from the Internal Revenue Service may be required.

Valuation: Both the New Jersey Transfer Inheritance Tax Branch and the Internal Revenue Service value listed securities in accordance with the quotations available in the financial sections of the daily newspapers. The unlisted security requires special valuation procedures.

To sell or not: The decision depends on the condition of the company which issued the particular stock or bond in question, such as its history, present balance sheet position, earnings capacity, as well as the general assets and liability picture of your estate and the needs of the beneficiaries.

25. Stocks (Unlisted)

The usual case involves the stock of a *closely held corporation*, or *small business*, or perhaps the *family business*. Quotations are not available in the newspapers. Hence the need for an independent appraisal as to the value.

Who does it? The appraisal can be performed by the person who possesses the necessary expertise. In some cases the accountant, public or certified, who has done the books for the company, can prepare the necessary financial history for the New Jersey Transfer Inheritance Branch and the Internal Revenue Service. There are also many professional appraisal firms, some of which even specialize in the type of company or field involved, who perform this type of service.

How is it done? The valuation of unlisted closely held stock depends on the type of business, its history, its balance sheets and profit and loss statements for the past several years, its competition, and its future potential earnings. These several factors help determine the stock's market value. This question of valuation is a highly specialized area.

26. Business Interests

Your business interests will probably consist of stock in a small, closely-held **corporation**, or a **small business**, or **family business**, or a **partnership**, or proprietorship.

Valuation is the same as that for unlisted stocks (previously discussed) - appraisal by the accountant or other independent expert.

If your will left any instructions as to what should be done with these business interests or if before you died you signed an agreement as to what should be done with these business interests, the duties and steps to follow of the Personal Representative should be clear.

On the other hand, the Personal Representative will have the responsibility of deciding to **continue** your business or **liquidate** or **sell** it. The factors which comprise such a decision include the condition of your business, its prospects, and the needs and desires of the beneficiaries.

Note: The Personal Representative is empowered by law to continue your business, but if it is to be continued **after your estate is wound up is another matter.** The stock can be transferred. The partnership (assuming there is no agreement made during your life) may be automatically dissolved on your death as a matter of law; and if the partnership and/or the proprietorship are to be continued, it will probably have to be done by some kind of successor business entity.

In any event the Personal Representative will have to take the steps necessary to preserve your business. This means familiarizing himself with it as soon as possible.

27. Tangible Personal Property

The automobile was previously discussed; but the rest of your *tangible personal property* includes your clothing, jewelry, furniture and the like.

The significant, worthwhile items, such as the gold watch, the grand piano, and the yacht, will have to be appraised. There are experts who specialize in this area. If they cannot give an accurate appraisal, then they usually can find somebody who can.

Again, it is the Personal Representative who has the duty to locate your personal property, take good care of it, have it appraised, decide whether to sell it or give it away (often the Salvation Army can use your old clothes) or see that any proper instructions under your will are carried out.

28. Estate Property Outside New Jersey

The most usual situation is when you or you and your spouse own real property which is situated in another state. However, estate property outside New Jersey may also include tangible and intangible personal property (such as an out of state bank account).

The Personal Representative, through his attorney, must review the law of the state (or country) in which your property is located to see how it can be transferred to the proper beneficiary and to see if it may be subject to the estate or inheritance tax laws, if any, of such other state or country.

Estate property outside New Jersey may have to be administered in such state or country by procedure similar to the administration of estate property in New Jersey. This special procedure is often referred to as **Ancillary Administration**. Simply put, the Personal Representative obtains Letters of Administration or Letters Testamentary (or the equivalent of them) in such state or country, in accordance with its special laws and procedures, and acts accordingly.

If a tax is due such other state or country, the Personal Representative must prepare and file the appropriate returns.

29. Income Tax Returns

1. **Personal.** The tax year for most people is from January 1 to December 31. If you had income from January 1 until the date of your death, the Personal Representative will have to file personal federal and state income tax returns. If you and your spouse filed a joint return, the Personal Representative has the power to sign a joint return with your spouse. The return is usually due by April 15th of the following year.

2. **Estate.** If the estate has any income, be it from interest on bank deposits, dividends on stocks, or capital gains from the sale of stocks or other assets, the Personal Representative may have to file federal and state **fiduciary** income tax returns for each fiscal year during the life of the estate. In many cases this is done with the assistance of a certified public accountant or other tax expert.

   If the estate is expected to receive income, the Personal Representative, by completing and filing with the Internal Revenue Service a rather simple IRS Form SS-4, obtains a special tax identification number which is then used in the filing of returns.

Estate Income Tax Rates. After subtracting from gross income certain exemptions and deductions, which will not be set forth here, the tax is computed. Rates are as follows:

If the taxable income is:	but not over	The tax is
$ 0	$1,800	15%
$1,800	$4,250	$270 + 27.5%
$4,250	$6,500	$943.75 + 30.5%
$6,500	$8,900	$1,630 + 35.5%
$8,900	-------	$2,482 + 39.1%

New Jersey does not tax income of $10,000 or less. The rates over $10,000 are as follows:

If the taxable income is:	The tax is:
Not over $20,000	1.4% of taxable income
Over $20,000 but not over $35,000	1.75% less $70.00
Over $35,000 but not over $40,000	3.5% less $682.50
Over $40,000 but not over $75,000	5.5525% less $1,492.50
Over $75,000	6.37% less $2,126.25

30. Inventories

The filing of an ***inventory*** with the court does not occur often. However, its procedure should be discussed here.

What is it? It is an itemization, together with values, of what you owned at the time of your death. It is filed with the court if required by court order or if desired at the discretion of the Personal Representative or demanded by any interested party or if there is to be an exemption for the benefit of your family.

The Exemption. Unless your will directs otherwise, your wearing apparel and your personal property to the value of $5,000.00 is reserved for the use of your family and is exempt from the claims of your creditors. To arrive at this exempt value the inventory procedure is followed.

The procedure of making and filing an inventory involves the selection, subject to court approval, of two appraisers who then itemize and value your property. The inventory is then filed with the court under oath (in affidavit form) by the Personal Representative and at least one of the appraisers to the effect that your property was appraised at its true value according to their best judgment.

With respect to the exemption the Personal Representative or surviving widow (the law does not say widower) may select property up to $5,000.00. Such property becomes exempt property for the family use.

31. Accounting

What is it? It is the Personal Representative's formal statement as to what happened to your estate.

The accounting recites every property item together with its value which came into the possession of the Personal Representative after you died. It tells what happened to all the property - whether it was retained or sold and, if so, for how much, whether it earned income and, if so, how much, whether and when it was distributed to beneficiaries and, if so, the value at the date of distribution. It also tells what debts and taxes were paid and what claims were collected. And there is also included those matters pertaining to fees and commissions of attorneys, accountants, and the Personal Representative.

Is an accounting always required? The Personal Representative must tell the beneficiaries what happened to the estate assets and liabilities; so to that extent the answer is ***yes***. As to whether the Personal Representative must always file a ***formal account*** with the court, the answer is ***no*** - not if all beneficiaries, who must all be mentally competent adults, agree in writing and give the Personal Representative a formal written release or discharge.

When is an accounting required? There is no real time limit. However, the Personal Representative is not required to account until at least one year after his appointment. The Personal Representative may render intermediate accounts during the course of the administration of your estate or one final account.

How is the accounting rendered? If it is an ***informal accounting***, the Personal Representative sends his statement to all beneficiaries for approval. If it is a formal accounting, the Personal Representative goes to court to get the accounting formally approved. All beneficiaries are notified. They have the right to go to court and object to any portion of the accounting and examine the Personal Representative under oath. If there is no problem, the court approves the accounting as well as commissions, counsel fees and other expenses.

Note: There are certain instances where a beneficiary may require the Personal Representative to account. See later discussion under Discharge of the Personal Representative at page 62.

---

32. Commissions Of The Personal Representative

First, you may in your will fix the specific compensation of the Personal Representative. However, the Personal Representative may, in a writing filed with the court, renounce any such will provision.

Income Commissions: On all ***income*** of the estate which the Personal Representative receives, the commission is 6%.

Corpus Commissions: On all **corpus**, or **principal** of the estate - that is, the body of the estate itself --

5% of the first $200,000.

3½% on the excess of $200,000 up to $1,000,000.

2% on the excess over $1,000,000.

With two or more Personal Representatives the commissions are the same as above and in addition thereto 1% of all corpus for each additional Personal Representative, provided that no one Personal Representative can take no more than an individual Personal Representative.

However, a court may reduce the commissions if a beneficiary can show that the services rendered were deficient or that the pain, trouble and risk were substantially less than generally required for similar estates.

33. Attorneys' Fees

For services rendered the attorney is entitled to a reasonable fee based upon such factors as the amount of time spent and the degree of difficulty of the problems encountered. When a formal accounting is rendered the fee requested by the attorney is subject to the approval of the court.

Problem: At the beginning of administration it can be difficult to estimate what the counsel fee will be. Moreover, in some popular literature there has been much criticism of the fees charged and collected and approved by courts in New Jersey and elsewhere. Some of this criticism is justified. The best guidance on the first visit to the attorney is to find out what may be involved as far as time and hourly rates are concerned, and if the answer forthcoming is not direct, then to seek assistance elsewhere.

Note: The attorney who prepared the will is not automatically entitled to get the estate (even if the will says so). This decision remains with the Executor.

34. Managing The Estate - Investments

Any Fiduciary (Executor, Trustee, and Guardian has the duty to **manage your estate** in such a way that its **value is preserved** and not permitted to waste. Unless your will directs otherwise, the Fiduciary may very well face the issues of investing and reinvesting some of the assets of your estate.

New Jersey's **Prudent Investment Act** sets certain standards of "reasonable care, skill and caution..." These include "considering the purposes, terms, distributions and other circumstances" of the assets, and in investing the money and property of your estate, exercising "care and judgment under the circumstances..."; and some of the circumstances to be considered include general economic conditions, the possible effect of inflation or deflation, tax consequences, the expected total return, the need for liquidity, the wisdom of diversifying, and so on. As to what is **prudent** will depend on the facts and circumstances of each particular situation.

If the Fiduciary is unsure about a certain investment - whether to make it or not - he may seek outside counsel, even from the court.

Abandonment of Real Property. The Personal Representative may in some instances apply to the court for an order permitting him to abandon any real property interest in your estate if because of so many mortgages and other such legal encumbrances and liens or because of lack of income it is not worth preserving.

35. Discharge Of The Personal Representative

At any time after appointment, the Personal Representative may be discharged by the court for sufficient cause or reason. **Grounds for discharge** include:

1. Failure to account to the beneficiaries and/or the court as to the assets and liabilities and status of any other matter of the estate when required to do so.

2. Failure to post a bond when required to do so.

3. Deliberate refusal or neglect to obey any order of the court.

4. Embezzlement or waste or misapplication of part or all of the estate asset.

5. Abuse of trust and confidence, such as conflict of interest transactions.

6. Deliberate refusal or neglect to proceed with the administration of the estate and/or deliberate refusal or neglect to perform any duties.

7. Unsound mind or mental capacity.

8. Hindering or preventing the administration of the estate.

If any person (usually a beneficiary) believes the Personal Representative should be discharged, a complaint is filed, the Personal Representative is given notice of the charges, and a court hearing is held.

A Personal Representative who is discharged for cause forfeits his rights to any and all commissions. And, as previously stated, if a Personal Representative has committed a wrongful act, he can be sued individually.

36. Distribution

Procedure. The Personal Representative delivers to the beneficiary the share you left him or her in your will and takes back from that beneficiary a Release and Refunding Bond which the Personal Representative then files with the Surrogate.

The **Release and Refunding Bond** is a special document which recites receipt of the share, release of the Personal Representative from liability, and states that if all or any part of the share is needed to pay any further debts or claims of the estate and the Personal Representative does not have any money to pay those debts or claims, then the beneficiary will return enough money from the share to the Personal Representative so that the debts and claims can be paid.

Additionally:

1. An undistributed money bequest bears interest beginning one year after the Personal Representative is appointed and ending on the date of distribution (unless your will directs otherwise).

2. If a beneficiary is due a share and the Personal Representative refuses to distribute it, the beneficiary can sue the Personal Representative.

3. Subject to certain conditions, the Personal Representative may distribute a share in cash or in kind (property having a value equivalent to the share - unless your will directs otherwise).

4. If beneficiaries cannot be located (the Personal Representative does not know who they are and/or where they are), then the Personal Representative may obtain from the court an order to notify them by means

of a publication of such notice in a newspaper, and if they fail to respond, their interests may be barred.

If there are insufficient remaining assets in your estate (and no instructions in your will as to what to do in such a case), then the **order of satisfaction** or **preference** is as follows:

a. Specific bequests (certain property, such as your piano or ring).

b. General bequests (sums of money to certain individuals).

c. The residuary (the rest or remainder of your estate).

d. Intestacy (when your will has been silent in part with respect to a beneficiary and New Jersey law determines who that beneficiary is).

Note: If there are insufficient assets for beneficiaries in any of the above classes, then those beneficiaries share **pro rata** (in equal percentages).

---

37. The Minor And Guardianship

A **minor** is a person under the age of 18 years.

Note: There are exceptions. Marriage can change minority status. Moreover, the **Uniform Gifts to Minors Act**, discussed later, classifies minors as those persons under 21 years of age.

There are two kinds of **Guardians** – the **Guardian of the Person** and the **Guardian of the Estate**. The Guardian of the Person is entrusted with the care and custody of the minor. The Guardian of the Estate is entrusted with the handling and management of the property of the minor.

The same person can be, and many times is, ***both Guardian of the Person and Guardian of the Estate***. Guardians who handle the property of a minor, be they Guardians of the Person or Guardians of the Estate, are held to the same standards as are Personal Representatives of the estate. They have the same responsibility, subject to court supervision.

During the course of the administration of your estate, a minor who is a beneficiary ordinarily must have a ***Guardian of the Person*** and a ***Guardian of the Estate***, and the logical or leading choice is the parent (in the case of your children, the ***surviving*** parent). In your will you may appoint the Guardian, and you may also direct that such Guardian serve without the necessity of posting a bond.

> Note: If in your will you appoint a Guardian for your child who is a person other than such child's other parent, then such Guardianship will not become effective after your death unless such other parent consents.

If there is no surviving parent, and if you do not appoint a Guardian in your will, then the court will appoint some other person who may or may not be related to you but who will probably best suit the interests and needs of the minor under all the circumstances. (A responsible relative who knows the child is preferred.)

Guardianship involves the ***management*** and ***application*** of the ***income*** and ***principal*** of the minor's property for his support, care and education.

Guardianship ends upon the minor's death, adoption, marriage, or attainment of the age of 18 years, at which time the Guardian must pay and distribute to the minor all his money and property.

There is, however, an exception to the above Guardianship requirements: If a Guardian of the estate has not been appointed, the Personal Representative may distribute to such minor money or property up to $5,000 in any one year. Distribution shall only be made as follows:

1. To the minor directly but only if married.

2. To the minor's parent or parents.

3. To any adult person who has general care and custody of the minor and with whom the minor is living.

4. To the Guardian of the person of the minor.

5. To a federally insured savings account in the sole name of the minor.

38. Commissions Of The Guardian

Commissions of the Guardian. They are as follows:

Income Commissions: On all **income** of the minor's estate which the Guardian receives, the commission is 6%.

Corpus Commissions: On all **corpus**, or **principal** of the minor's estate - that is, the body of the minor's estate itself - the Guardian may take **annual commissions** as follows:

1. 5/10 of 1% (or .005) of the first $400,000.

2. 3/10 of 1% (or .003) on amounts in excess of $400,000.

Additionally: At the end of the guardianship or on distribution of any assets from the minor's estate:

3. Those corpus commissions in the above amounts due but not yet taken or received by the Guardian; and

4. If the guardianship is terminated or part of the corpus is distributed, that percentage of corpus actually distributed (in whole or in part) within the following time period:

    a. Within 5 years after the guardianship began: 2%.

    b. Between 5 to 10 years after the guardianship began: 1½%.

    c. More than 20 years after the guardianship began: 1%.

And a court may allow even additional corpus commissions if the Guardian has rendered unusual or extraordinary services.

39. The Incapacitated Beneficiary

The beneficiary who, by reason of mental infirmity, age, feeble-mindedness, etc., is unable to manage his affairs is subject to similar principles of guardianship as those previously discussed for minors.

Your will may designate a Guardianship. However, if in your will you appoint a Guardian for a beneficiary who is not declared by a court to be incapacitated, then before such person can be made a full Guardian, the court must adjudicate the entire issue of mental competency.

This usually takes place with the affidavits or testimony of two medical physicians at a full court hearing with notice to all interested parties who have the right to appear and be heard.

40. How Long Does Administration Take?

It depends.

If you die without a will, then the time for administration can be no less than one year provided that, if the six-month Notice to Creditors previously discussed has been properly given, then the time for administration may end after the conclusion of such six-month period.

Otherwise, administration may take as little as a few months or as long as several years. Some reasons for delay include:

1. Difficulty in locating a beneficiary.

2. Litigation of such issues as the validity or interpretation of your will, the valuation of some of your assets, the discharge of the Personal Representative. Parties to litigation sometimes include creditors, beneficiaries, taxing authorities (the New Jersey Transfer Inheritance Tax Branch or the Internal Revenue Service).

   Example: The Personal Representative and the Internal Revenue Service cannot agree as to the value of your business for federal estate tax purposes. The matter is litigated. If it ends up in the United States Tax Court, it could take a few years. If it ends up in the United States Supreme Court, it could take several years.

3. Procrastination of the Personal Representative or the attorney for the estate or arguments between or among beneficiaries.

Note: Despite the above, administration does not always have to be the long, expensive, cumbersome process many people, for one reason or another, have made it out to be.

Example: You leave your entire estate to your wife and appoint her Executrix. Your assets consist of property which is easily transferrable and which has a quickly ascertainable value (a listed security, a bank account). Your estate has little or no income. The administration of your estate should take a few months at the most and with minimal expenses.

PART IV:
ESTATE PLANNING

1. *Estate Planning*

What is it?

It is the arrangement you make with your property to make sure that when you die it goes to the beneficiaries you want, in the form you want, and at the lowest estate and inheritance tax rates and estate administration costs. Estate planning also includes making available at your death sufficient liquid funds with which to pay your estate debts and costs.

Your ***property*** includes your assets:

1. Your real property.

2. Your tangible personal property, such as your car, piano, jewelry.

3. Your intangible property, such as your stocks, bonds, life insurance, bank accounts, retirement funds, rights under any claims against others.

The ***beneficiaries*** you want are simply the persons or institutions to whom you want your property to go. If you die without a will, your property may not go to the beneficiaries you want.

To the beneficiaries you want ***in the form you want*** introduces a new concept not mentioned before - the ***trust***. You may want some or all of your beneficiaries to have your property *in trust* rather than *outright*. This will be discussed shortly.

At the lowest estate and inheritance (and even income) *tax rates* and *administration costs*: You want to leave *as much of your property as possible* to your beneficiaries by paying *the lowest possible taxes and costs* but note: The two goals of leaving your property to the people you want in the form you want and saving taxes and costs may not always be compatible. For example, because of the federal estate tax marital deduction, it will cost you less to leave the vacation house you own in your name alone to your wife, but for one or more reasons you may insist on leaving it to your son. (Fine, as long as it is a conscious decision you make with full knowledge of the estate tax consequences.)

Estate planning includes the use of some or all or some combination of the tools and techniques discussed in the following.

2. The Will

As briefly discussed before, your will can designate who receives what and how as well as who administers your estate and cares for your children. Now for a more detailed discussion of this obviously important estate planning tool.

1. *The introduction*. You recite who you are and where you live and that what you are making is your will.

Note: Where you state you live is not always controlling; it depends where you *actually lived* at the time of your death.

Example: You make your will while living in California, recite in your will that you live in California, then sell your home in California, move to New Jersey, purchase a home in New Jersey, live in New Jersey for ten years, then die in New Jersey. Despite what you said in your will, you died a resident of New Jersey. For all purposes, tax and other, your estate will be administered in New Jersey.

2. ***Burial instructions***. You do not have to recite these in your will. You may instead write them out and give them to a friend or relative. However, if you have definite ideas on the subject, then it is wise to include them in your will.

3. ***The payment of your just debts***. A direction in your will that your Executor pay your just debts as well as the expenses of your last illness is usually redundant because that is what New Jersey law requires in any event. However, there are exceptions, not discussed here, which may pertain to your individual situation.

4. ***The payment of inheritance and estate taxes***. The designation as to which part of your estate - or which of your assets - is to be responsible for the payment of your inheritance and estate taxes could in some instances save on the amount of taxes due. Moreover, the New Jersey Transfer Inheritance Tax is imposed on the beneficiaries of your estate. You may wish to instruct that your estate should pay these taxes.

5. ***The bequest of any (or all) of your personal property***. This simply means you leave your piano to your nephew, your gold watch to your son, and the rest of your tangible personal property to your spouse. Not only does this bequest carry out your intent, but there may be a tax advantage:

If you leave a beneficiary your entire estate in one will clause instead of two will clauses, such as a bequest of your tangible personal property to that beneficiary ***and*** a bequest of all the rest of your estate to that beneficiary, then, for technical reasons, there may be an income tax to pay on the value of the tangible personal property disposed of in the one will clause case but not in the two will clauses case.

73

You may bequeath ***intangible*** as well as ***tangible*** personal property: To your nephew your one hundred shares of General Motors common stock.

6. ***The bequest of any (or all) of your real property.*** (This does not include the real estate you own jointly with another with right of survivorship.) ***Example***: You and your brother own a home at the seashore. If you do not own it as ***joint tenants with right of survivorship*** (and the deed will say so), then you own it as ***tenants in common***, which means that each of you owns a one-half interest and you may will such one-half interest to whomever you wish.

Note: If you bequeath real property which is encumbered by a mortgage, you may wish to specify whether or how that mortgage is to be paid out of your estate assets.

---

7. ***The bequest of specific amounts of money.*** The sum of $200.00 to your nephew, $500.00 to your son, and so on.

8. ***The exercise of a Power of Appointment. Example***: Another person who died before you did may have left you certain property together with the right on your part to specify in your will to what person or institution such property should go when you die. Such right on your behalf is a ***Power of Appointment***. This is often a difficult concept to grasp as well as a difficult estate planning tool to use.

9. ***The forgiveness of a debt***. Your nephew may have borrowed $500.00 from you and in return gave you a promissory note. This $500.00, or any part of which is unpaid at the time of your death, is an asset of your estate. Nonetheless, if you so desire, you may in your will forgive your nephew this debt.

10. ***Disposition of your business interests***. If your business interests consist of a corporation, you may dispose of the stock you own by way of a will provision. Moreover, if you own a partnership or proprietorship interest, you may likewise dispose of it in your will with instructions as to its continuance or discontinuance. (If you do not so direct, then the Personal Representative has the right to continue your business until it is wound up.)

11. ***The bequest of the rest of your estate***. The residue or remainder of your estate consists of everything left over after making all the above bequests. So in the above provisions, you designate the beneficiary or beneficiaries and the extent to which they share.

What if a beneficiary dies before your do? Then you may specify in your will how such beneficiary's share will be disposed of.

Note: If you do not so specify, the laws of New Jersey may so specify. ***Example***: You leave everything to your spouse, who dies before you do. You die, leaving no children. Your estate passes under the laws of New Jersey as if you had died without a will.

---

12. ***The appointment of the Executor, Trustee, or Guardian***. You may in your will choose who will be your Executor, the Trustee of any trusts (discussed later), or Guardian of any of your children. In case anyone so appointed dies before you do or is unable or unwilling to serve, then your will may name a substitute or successor. You may also appoint more than one person to these positions.

13. ***Powers of the Executor, Trustee, or Guardian***. The laws of New Jersey have set forth extensive powers for Executors, Trustees, or Guardians (all these persons

are called **Fiduciaries**). In your will you may expand or limit these powers.

3. The Uniform Simultaneous Death Law

Almost all the states have adopted the **Uniform Simultaneous Death Law** to cover the so-called common disaster, where you and another die in such circumstances so that the question as to which of you died first cannot be answered. The common disaster is rare, but it does occur. **Example**: An airline tragedy.

When there is a common disaster between two people - say, you and your spouse - and the passing of your estate and your spouse's estate depends upon who died first, then under the Uniform Simultaneous Death Law your estate is administered as if you survived your spouse, and your spouse's estate is administered as if your spouse survived you.

Example: Your will leaves everything to your spouse. Your will further provides that if your spouse dies before you do, then everything goes to your children. You and your spouse then die instantaneously in an airplane crash. Under the Uniform Simultaneous Death Law it is presumed that in this airplane crash your spouse died before you did. Hence, based on this presumption, your estate passes directly to your children.

Problem: Under the above example, your estate may pay more federal estate taxes then necessary.

Solution: Your will may change the result in the examples by providing that in the event of a common disaster your spouse survived you. So may such other estate planning tools as the trust and the life insurance policy.

Note: With respect to the life insurance policy, the Uniform Simultaneous Death Law provides that in the event of a common disaster, the insured is presumed to have survived the beneficiary. If you are the insured, then the proceeds of life insurance under such a situation could become payable to your estate and this may be subject to the New Jersey Transfer Inheritance Tax (unless the policy provided otherwise).

Other Applicable Situations: Successive beneficiaries and joint tenants with right of survivorship.

4.   The Anatomical Gift Act

You may give all or any part of your body to any hospital, surgeon or physician or medical school or storage facility for research or transplant.

If you do not make such a gift, then when you die these persons in the following order of priority shall have the right to do so: your spouse, adult son, daughter, parent, brother, sister, guardian or any other person authorized to dispose of your body.

You may make the ***gift by will*** or by another ***written document*** signed by you and two witnesses. you may even make the gift by means of a tape recording (in your voice) or by a card (signed and witnessed) carried on your person.

5.   The Living Will And The Natural Death Act

New Jersey Supreme Court decisions, as well as the media, focused public attention on those situations in which a person's life is prolonged only by artificial means. The decision to withhold or withdraw life sustaining procedures and equipment is, to say the least, a most difficult one, especially if no one knows the desires of the comatose patients.

Hence the Medical Directive or so-called "living will," a document which you may sign and have witnessed and which recites that if you ever are in a comatose or vegetative state that you desire not to be kept alive by artificial means.

On January 7, 1992, a new law was enacted: The New Jersey Advance Directives for Health Care Act, which enables you to set forth in writing your desires and/or to appoint someone to act on your behalf.

6. *The Trust And Its Purpose*

The previous discussion implied outright **bequests** to beneficiaries, but you may not want to do this. **Trust bequests** are an important part of estate planning.

The trust is a special form of property ownership explained as follows:

Suppose you own 100 shares of stock trading at $10.00 per share and paying an annual dividend of $1.00 per share. You are the sole and absolute owner of that stock. You can sell it, borrow money against it, or give it away.

Suppose you decide to give the stock to your brother. If so, then he becomes the sole and absolute owner of it. He can sell it, borrow money against it, or give it away.

But suppose you decide to create a trust for the stock. Suppose that, instead of giving the stock to your brother outright, you give it to him by way of a trust. How is this done?

You give the stock to a third person, a **Trustee**, for **the benefit of** your brother. With a trust, your brother is not the sole and absolute owner of the stock, and neither is the Trustee. Instead the sole and absolute ownership is divided into two parts:

1. The Trustee is the legal owner.

2. Your brother is the beneficial owner.

The sum of the legal ownership and beneficial ownership of the stock equals the sole and absolute ownership. Together, the Trustee and your brother as beneficiary are the sole and absolute owners of the stock.

Why might you want to give the stock to the Trustee for the benefit of your brother instead of to your brother outright? For perhaps some of the following reasons:

1. Your brother may be ***mentally*** or ***physically*** incapacitated. He is unable to exercise sole and absolute ownership of the stock the way a normal person could. You want him to have the benefit of the stock but you also want the ownership managed by someone else.

2. Your brother may be a ***minor***. Hence he would be prohibited by law from exercising full ownership. The function of the Trustee in this instance would be similar to that of the Guardian of the estate of a minor as previously discussed.

Your brother should not have full ownership of the stock because ***he might not manage it for his best interests***. He may, for example, have a severe, compulsive gambling problem.

Creating a trust may be a way for you to ***save on estate*** and/or ***income taxes***.

In the above situations, you give your property in trust - to a ***Trustee***, who manages it for the benefit of a ***beneficiary***.

7. Management Of The Trust

As the creator of the trust you can direct how the trust can be managed. Your instructions may include how the trust **income** (the dividend of $1.00 per share) and principal (the 100 shares of stock itself valued at $10.00 per share) can be managed.

1. You may direct that the Trustee pay the **income** to your brother for as long as the trust lasts. The income may be paid in periodic installments (monthly, quarterly, annually). Or you may direct that the Trustee only pay your brother part of the income - enough, say, only for your brother's welfare as the Trustee determines - and accumulate the income not paid to your brother and add it to trust principal.

2. You may direct that the Trustee pay your brother **none** of the trust principal. Or you may direct that the Trustee pay your brother **part** of the trust **principal** - enough, say, only for your brother's support or education or welfare, and only if the trust income is insufficient - either with shares of the stock or by selling the stock and paying cash.

3. You may direct that the Trustee **do nothing** with the trust principal - that is, hold on to the stock. Or you may direct that the Trustee manage and invest and reinvest the trust principal, so that, if the Trustee determines it is necessary or wise, he may sell the stock and purchase another security or a bond or hold the trust principal in cash.

4. You may direct **how long the trust shall last** - for one year or ten years or for the remainder of your brother's life.

5. You may direct **what happens to the trust at the end of its term**. You may want the trust to last for ten years.

At the end of ten years, the Trustee pays all the principal and all undistributed income to your brother. At that time, your brother becomes the sole and absolute owner of the 100 shares of stock. Or you may want the stock to last for your brother's life and then have the principal and undistributed income paid to his children or have the trust continued for the benefit of your sister.

6. You may add **other terms to the trust**. Some examples:

    a. It is common to add a **spendthrift provision**. If, for example, your brother is a compulsive gambler, you may instruct, when you establish the trust, that none of your brother's creditors may satisfy their claims against your brother by acquiring trust principal and/or income.

    b. You may also give the beneficiary (in the example above, your brother), a **power of appointment**, with the right on his part to direct how trust principal and income are to be disposed of in the event of his death. **Example**: You give the stock to the Trustee for the benefit of your brother for the life of your brother, and when he dies the trust principal and income shall be disposed of in accordance with the provisions of your brother's will. It is said that you have given your brother a **power of appointment**.

8. *Powers And Duties Of The Trustee*

Like the Personal **Representative** and the **Guardian**, the **Trustee** is a **Fiduciary**. Hence he has the same **powers** as described before and repeated now (unless limited or expanded by the terms of the trust): To accept additions to the trust, to invest and reinvest the assets, to keep insurance policies in force, to possess, manage and sell real and personal property, to employ and compensate attorneys, to settle claims for or against the trust, to enter into contracts.

The same **duties** apply to the Trustee as to any other Fiduciary. They include the standards of **prudent investment** and **reasonable care**. Moreover, from time to time the Trustee must account to the beneficiary and, if required, to the court (unless the beneficiary relinquishes such right by giving the Trustee a formal release).

As previously stated, the beneficiary's interest in the trust is less than full and absolute ownership. It is one of **beneficial ownership**, which gives the beneficiary the right to have the Trustee manage the trust properly and account to him. Also, the grounds and procedure for **discharge** of a Personal Representative - dishonesty, mismanagement and the like, as previously discussed - apply as well to the Trustee.

9. Types of Trusts

1. **Testamentary.** You create the trust in your will. Example: Instead of giving your nephew 100 shares of General Motors common stock you give your Trustee 100 shares of General Motors common stock. You empower your Trustee to pay the income (the dividends) of the stock to your nephew until he attains the age of 25 years, at which time the Trustee delivers the stock to your nephew and the trust ends.

2. **Lifetime.** This is also known as the Inter Vivos trust. Instead of setting the trust up in your will, you set it up before you die. You place the 100 shares of stock into trust and begin having your Trustee make the income payments from it while you are still alive.

3. **Irrevocable.** The trust established by will, or the **Testamentary Trust**, is by its nature irrevocable. It takes effect upon your death and you are not around

to revoke it. (Unless by the original terms it is to last for a certain number of years and then revert back to your estate. Unlikely.) What is usually meant by an *irrevocable trust is a trust established in your lifetime*, an *Inter Vivos Trust*, which in its original terms states it cannot be revoked by you. It can never end and its assets can never come back to you or your estate.

4. *Revocable*. The revocable trust, on the other hand, may be revoked by you at any time or at a specific time, and its assets revert to you or your estate.

10. Commissions Of The Trustee

They are as follows:

Income Commissions: On all *income* of the trust which the Trustee received, the commission is 6%.

Corpus Commissions: On all corpus, or principal of the trust - that is, the body of the trust itself - the Trustee may take annual commissions as follows:

1. 5/10 of 1% (or .005) of the first $400,000.

2. 3/10 of 1% (or .003) on amounts in excess of $400,000.

Additionally: At the end of the trust or on the distribution of any assets from the trust:

1. Those corpus commissions in the above amounts due but not yet taken or received, *and*:

2. If the trust is terminated or part of the corpus is distributed, that percentage of corpus actually distributed (in whole or in part) within the following time period:

a. Within 5 years after the trust began: 2%.

b. Between 5 to 10 years after the trust began: 1½%.

c. More than 10 years after the trust began: 1%.

And a court may allow even additional corpus commissions if the Trustee has rendered unusual or extraordinary services.

Note:

When you have **appointed a Trustee under your will and set a specific compensation**, the Trustee shall accept that compensation unless he renounces it in a writing filed with the court.

When you have **appointed a Trustee under a living or Inter Vivos** trust and set a specific compensation, then the Trustee shall accept that compensation. But if you have not set that compensation, then the above percentages apply.

---

11. The Use Of The Trust

This was briefly mentioned before: The trust is useful when the beneficiary, for one reason or another, cannot or should not have sole and absolute ownership - someone underage or incapacitated or careless with money.

The trust has other uses:

1. As a way to avoid probate. **You may establish a trust while you are alive** - *a* living *or* inter vivos **trust**. You may transfer property to the trust while you are alive. Or you may make a pourover will, which leaves your entire estate to the Trustee of the trust, to be administered and distributed in accordance with the terms of the trust.

In any event the costs and expenses of probate, not to mention the time involved, are eliminated or diminished. If you transfer all your property to the trust while you are alive, there is nothing left in your estate when you die. You thus leave no estate to be administered.

Note: Avoiding probate does not necessarily mean avoiding inheritance and estate taxes.

---

2. ***As a way to protect your loved ones***. This does not just mean the brother who is the compulsive gambler. This also means your spouse who has no desire or ability to manage money. It also means all the members of your entire family. For example, you may establish a trust for the benefit of your spouse and children and instruct the Trustee to distribute the income and principal in such proportions, without regard to equality of distribution, to those beneficiaries who need it most. This is known as a ***sprinkling trust***.

3. ***As a way to protect your business***. The smooth transition of both ownership and management aspects of your business can be accomplished by the use of the trust. If you do not have a trust, or some other sort of lifetime arrangement, such as a "buy-sell" agreement, which will be discussed later, then the administration of your business interest as a probate asset could cause problems in the areas of valuation for tax purposes, management and continuance, and transfer of ownership.

4. ***As a way to minimize estate taxes***. As previously stated, you may, because of a federal estate tax provision known as the marital deduction, leave your entire estate to your spouse tax free. But when your spouse eventually dies, the federal estate tax will be imposed on his or her entire estate. This will include your spouse's estate and the unconsumed portion of the estate you left your spouse. The use of a trust or

trusts, in very special ways, for the benefit of your spouse and other family members, may be able to reduce this federal estate tax burden.

Note: The New Jersey Transfer Inheritance Tax has no marital deduction.

Moreover, the transfer of **life insurance policies** to an irrevocable trust (an insurance trust) may also reduce federal estate taxes.

5. **As a way to minimize income taxes**. Although the savings in income taxes is outside the scope of this book, the subject should be mentioned. **Example**: Certain lifetime trusts can shift the income tax burden (and thus lower it) from you to your minor children.

12. Gifts

Giving your property away before you die is another estate planning tool. In this case, however, the beneficiary receives the property outright and exercises all incidents of complete ownership.

1. **You may avoid probate**. Contrary to what may be believed by many people, you commit no crime if you are on your deathbed and sign over to your son the bank account which is in your sole name. Although the Personal Representative will have to report the bank account on your New Jersey Transfer Inheritance Tax Return and on your federal estate tax return and may have to pay taxes on it, by way of the gift it has been effectively removed from your estate as a probate asset.

2. **You may avoid New Jersey Transfer Inheritance Taxes**. If you give property to another person and live for three years or more and then die, the value

of the property you gave away will not be included in your estate for New Jersey Transfer Inheritance Tax Purposes. If you give property to another person and die within three years, you will be deemed to have made a gift in contemplation of death, unless the Personal Representative can prove that when you made the gift you did not make it for the purpose of avoiding the tax. At times, as far as proof is concerned, this can be a very difficult issue.

3. ***You may avoid Federal Estate Taxes***. Federal estate tax law used to have the above-described contemplation of death rule but repealed it. (Except for gifts of life insurance and gifts where you retain some ownership incidents.) So if you make a gift before you die, its value will not be included in your estate for federal estate tax purposes.

However, consider the following:

1. If you make a gift before you die, the Internal Revenue Service imposes a ***gift tax***. The federal estate tax rates and credits were previously discussed. That portion of any credit used to reduce the gift tax will not be available to reduce the estate tax when you die. ***Nevertheless, to repeat: The gift of an asset removes it from probate and administration***.

2. ***The annual exclusion to the gift tax***. Regardless of (1), in any one year you may give, free of gift tax, to any single beneficiary, money or property worth up to $11,000. If your spouse joins with you (whether or not your spouse owns the property), the amount is doubled to $22,000. In subsequent years this amount may be adjusted for inflation. Furthermore, the ***gift tax*** does not apply when you pay someone else's tuition or medical expenses, provided payments are made directly to the educational institution or the medical provider.

Note: You may not want to make a gift. You may want to retain all or some control over the property (if you do, you haven't made a gift). Or you don't want the beneficiary to control the property. ***But***: A gift into an irrevocable trust in which you have retained no powers may accomplish your purpose.

Note: Gifts and bequests to ***charity*** are not subject to federal estate or gift tax or New Jersey Transfer Inheritance Tax.

13. The Uniform Gifts To Minors Act

This New Jersey law combines the principles of the gift and the trust.

Although New Jersey law generally defines an adult as being 18 years of age or more, the New Jersey Uniform Gifts to Minors Act defines an adult as being 21 years of age or more.

The kinds of property which you may give to a minor under this act are a security (such as stock), an insurance policy or annuity contract, tangible personal property, a partnership interest, or money.

You make the gift to an adult person known as a Custodian. The Custodian's powers and duties are very similar to those of the Trustee under a trust:

1. To collect, hold, manage, invest and reinvest the custodial property.

2. To use the custodial property for the support, maintenance, education, general use and benefit of the minor as the Custodian in his or her absolute discretion deems proper.

3. Within certain exceptions, to pay or transfer the property to the minor when he or she reaches the age of 21.

The custodian is held to similar standards of prudent investment and care as is the Trustee and can be made to account for dishonesty or mismanagement. Also, you may specify when you make the gift what kind of compensation the Custodian will receive, and if you do not, then the Custodian receives the same compensation as would the Guardian of a minor's estate.

Many times the Uniform Gifts to Minors Act may be used when (1) when you wish to make a gift and (2) you do not wish to establish a trust.

14. Joint Ownership

1. It avoids estate administration because upon your death the property passes outside your estate to the survivor or survivors.

2. Under New Jersey law, you are presumed - for New Jersey Transfer Inheritance Taxes - to have owned *all* the property at the time of your death. Unless the Personal Representative can prove the survivor paid for or contributed all or part of the property, its entire value will be included in your estate.

   Exception: Real property held by you and your spouse jointly with right of survivorship is exempt from the New Jersey Transfer Inheritance Tax. So, from an estate planning standpoint, if you own New Jersey real estate in your name alone, you avoid probate expense and transfer inheritance taxes by placing such property in the names of yourself and your spouse.

3. Under federal estate tax law, full taxation of the joint interest - or the inclusion of the full value of the property in your estate unless the Personal Representative can

prove the survivor paid for or contributed all or a part of the property depends on the following:

a. **For joint ownership between you and your spouse**, one half the interest in the property is included in your estate no matter which spouse furnished the contribution or payment.

b. **For joint ownership between you and other person not your spouse**, the entire interest in the property is included in your estate unless the Personal Representative can prove the survivor paid or contributed all or a part of the property.

Note: The federal income tax aspects of joint ownership between spouses is another factor to be considered.

Example: You and your spouse have owned real property jointly for several years. You die, and one-half the value of the property is included in your estate for federal estate tax purposes. But: If your spouse sells the property in the future and is required to report a capital gain, the cost basis of the property is as follows:

a. The one-half your spouse inherited on your death has a cost basis equivalent to one-half the entire value at the time of your death.

b. The other one-half has a cost basis equivalent to what was originally paid for the property.

15. The Power Of Attorney

The **Power of Attorney** is almost – **if not as** - important as **your will**. It is a document which empowers another person or persons to act on your behalf.

The Power of Attorney can be as limited or as general as you want it to be. It can cover the rental of a particular parcel of real property, or it can cover everything: giving the person you appoint - known as an **Attorney-in-Fact**, the power to do everything you could do if personally present, which includes: holding and selling property, depositing and withdrawing money from bank accounts, making personal decisions.

The Power of Attorney can be for a specified period of time such as a year, or you may designate that it remain in effect for an indefinite period of time until you revoke it. Moreover, you may specify that the Power of Attorney is to:

a.   become effective *only if you are disabled*, or

b.   remain effective *despite your becoming disabled*.

Why is the Power of Attorney so important?

If you become mentally or physically disabled (suppose you have a stroke) and you have not made a valid Power of Attorney, and there are decisions to be made and actions to be taken with regard to your business and personal affairs, then the court will have to appoint a Guardian.

The appointment of a Guardian can be a difficult, time-consuming and expensive process. Legal papers have to be prepared and filed with the court. You, or someone appointed on your behalf for the purpose of the court proceeding, must be notified of the hearing date set to determine whether you can manage your affairs. The affidavit or testimony as to your disability must be obtained from at least two physicians.

If at the time you become disabled there had been in existence a Power of Attorney made by you designating someone you wanted to act on your behalf, the whole guardianship procedure, with all its hassle, expense and delay, could be unnecessary.

16. *Estate Liquidity*

The purpose of **Estate Liquidity** is to make sure there are enough liquid funds in your estate at the time of your death or shortly after your death with which to pay estate administration expenses and taxes.

The problem of *illiquidity* can be acute and is perhaps illustrated by what could happen and does happen (for the most part in other areas of the country): If the chief asset in your estate is the family farm, when you die the Personal Representative may have to sell all or part of your farm in order to pay expenses and taxes. With respect to real estate (or a closely held business) finding a purchaser can be difficult. A sale may not occur for some time, and if it does, it may have to be at sacrifice prices.

Note: The Internal Revenue Code has relief provisions for these situations: In many of these situations the Personal Representative may extend the time for payment of the tax (free of penalty but not free of interest).

How to meet liquidity problems can be a difficult task. However, one answer can lie in obtaining sufficient life insurance.

17. *Agreements*

Estate planning also involves agreements you make during your life. Two important areas:

1. *The business agreement*. Whether you have stock in a small business corporation or a partnership or proprietorship interest, you may be able to simplify

ownership, management and liquidity problems through the use of an agreement with your business associates, and such agreements may include the use of life insurance.

Example: A buy-sell agreement with you and your partner funded with life insurance. Upon your death your partner collects enough insurance proceeds on your life to buy out your business interest. You have disposed of your business interest and obtained for your estate the necessary liquid cash.

Note: In the buy-sell agreement, if you have set a purchase price or provided for the means of setting a purchase price, then you may have fixed a value which the taxing authorities will accept when the Personal Representative files your transfer and inheritance tax returns. If this is the case, then you may have saved your estate much time and expense in arguing with the taxing authorities as to the value of your business.

2. ***The marriage agreement***. This agreement is usually advisable in the following situation: Two older people who have separate assets and families (widowed or divorced). They wish to marry but they want the members of their original families to have their assets; they do not wish to combine their assets, so they enter into a ***Pre-Marital*** or ***Ante-Nuptial*** agreement. It specifies the division of assets. They also make separate wills leaving their assets to their original family members.

Note: The right of the surviving spouse to take against the will, as previously discussed, may be voluntarily surrendered in this type of agreement. There should be no question as to the validity of this type of agreement if each person is represented by a separate attorney and there is full disclosure of all assets.

Note: A similar agreement may also be desirable for people living together but not contemplating marriage.

---

18. The Choice Of The Executor, Trustee And/Or Guardian

Should they be a person or persons you know or a bank? Answer: *It depends.*

1. If you have a small or moderate estate, together with a good marriage and trusting relatives who get on with each other, then *you may decide to select your spouse and others* whom you trust to be Executor, Trustee and/or Guardian. Even if you have a large estate which requires management experience, you may wish to rely on the selection of these people with the assurance that if they need assistance they will have the good sense to get it.

> Note: Even if the bank can do the better job, and that's no guarantee in the first place, circumstances may dictate the more suitable choice to be a trusted family relative.

2. *The bank may not always be familiar with particular personal family problems.* The bank may, however, be quite sensitive to these problems. Many decent trust officers, even if they have to power to act alone, will not act alone without first consulting the surviving spouse or beneficiary. And it may be the surviving spouse or some other relative who best knows the needs of your particular estate or family situation.

3. *A bank can provide management continuity.* Your spouse, who is your Executor, may die before your estate is wound up. This will not happen with a bank. Moreover, your bank may have the estate administration experience your spouse lacks.

4. *A bank can provide investment experience.* Your spouse may not know a single thing about managing your assets. A bank has an investment department.

But: bank investment track records may not always be spectacular. However, there is no harm in looking into this.

Possibility: The appointment of a family member and a bank as co-Executor or Trustee.

These are only some of the considerations in the selection of an Executor, Trustee and Guardian. But this really is part of a larger issue: the selection of qualified professionals (to be discussed at page 98).

19. Conclusion

The previous discussion is a ***very superficial*** glance at a very sophisticated, complex subject. To best illustrate this point, consider some topics ***not*** discussed: corporate recapitalizations, family partnerships, annuities, charitable giving, conservatorships, and even ***post mortem*** planning, which concerns some of the things which may be done after your death to facilitate administration, carry out your objectives, and minimize taxes. One useful post mortem tool is the ***disclaimer***: a beneficiary actually renounces ***all*** or part of a bequest.

Also, the treatment of many different questions and situations involving wills has by no means been exhaustive. There have been discussed and there have not been discussed several areas which require detailed professional analysis.

Finally, also not treated in this book have been such specialized topics as charitable bequests, the veteran, the mentally incapacitated child, and medicaid planning.

PART V:
ADDITIONAL POINTS

1. Can You Do The Job Yourself?

Yes. There is no law which prohibits you from making your own will and planning your own estate. And there is no law which requires you to have a will in the first place.

However: *Although you can do the job yourself, maybe you should not do the job yourself. It is so easy to botch it.*

The most important reason for *not* making your own will or planning your own estate is that this is a very difficult area - even for the experts. There is a significant risk you might make a *mistake* in the drafting of your will or planning of your estate so that it either does not go to whom you really want and/or its costs and taxes are much higher than they would have been had you had the proper guidance.

There are several reasons why people do not seek out the *proper professional help*:

1. *Superstition*. Many people are afraid that if they make a will they will die. This reason is obviously invalid.

2. *Indecision*. Either as to a *major point*, such as whom to name as beneficiary, or as to a *minor point*, such as whom to name as Guardian. Both these reasons are invalid. If you do not choose a beneficiary, the law will choose one for you when you die. And you can make

your will without naming a Guardian and name one later in a codicil to your will.

3. ***Ignorance***. Many people think they already know the law, which may be true; or they do not know the law and mistakenly believe they have already arranged their affairs for maximum benefit. Ignorance may or may not be bliss. But only a qualified professional can give the proper answer.

4. ***Mistrust***. Many people want to keep their personal affairs ***absolutely*** private. And they have ***no*** confidence in professional people. They may have a point: privacy is to be respected but, more important, finding a qualified and/or honest professional (unfortunately) can be a hit or miss thing. However, considering the potential risks involved in not seeking help - such as not having your estate go to whom you wish or having your estate incur unnecessary delay, costs and expenses - makes it probably worth your while to seek help.

5. ***Expense***. Many people, no matter how poor or wealthy, do not want to pay money to professionals. ***Valid but***: The expense incurred from paying professionals before you die may be much less than the expense your estate and your beneficiaries incur in paying professionals after you die - which, rightly or wrongly, may be the way you prefer it.

2. The Selection Of Qualified Professionals

You may have heard from extensive promotional literature about the "ideal" Estate Planning Team comprised of some combination of the attorney, the accountant, the trust officer from the bank, the insurance underwriter, the financial or estate planning consultant, and the account executive from the brokerage house.

Many of these people are competent, honest and (as far as fees are concerned) reasonable. On the other hand, some of these people are not qualified - even if they tell you they are (including attorneys).

Suggestion: The chances are you already ***know and trust*** one or more individuals in the above group of professionals. If so, seek them out and do not hesitate to ask them ***all*** the questions on your mind and give them ***all*** the information pertaining to your estate situation. If they don't have the answers to your situation they can probably guide you to those who do.

You will probably not need ***all*** the members of the ***Ideal Estate Planning Team***, but you will probably need at least one, the attorney, since the work to be done will involve the preparation of one or more legal documents.

You have a perfect right to ask at the outset how much all this work will cost. If an exact fee cannot be quoted, then you should at least be able to obtain a range of fees and/or an hourly rate and have all this put in writing.

If you know of no professional people to assist you, you may consider approaching the trust department of a bank - at no cost or obligation (and despite the size of your estate). Its representatives can recommend reputable attorneys, and if you do not like what you hear, then you may continue the search. Also, each county has a lawyer referral service (see Appendix, page 101). ***Many times there is no easy way to find qualified people***.

3. The Revision Of the Will And/Or Estate Plan

Everything has to be reviewed and possibly revised:

1. When family circumstances change.

2. When asset and liability situations change.

3. When the law changes.

4. When time marches on, which means *periodically* once every few years.

An extra expense? *Yes, but so is virtually everything.*

PART VI: APPENDIX

1. Some Surrogate Fees

Probate of Will and Letters Testamentary (up to two pages, $5.00 for each additional page)	$ 100.00
Probate of Codicil	50.00
Letters of Administration	125.00
Letters of Trusteeship	50.00
Letters of Guardianship	500.00
Accounting	
For filing and 1 page	175.00
In estates up to $2,000	no additional fee
In estates up to $2,000	no additional fee
In estates 2001 to $10,000	100.00
In estates 10,001 to $30,000	125.00
In estates 30,001 to $65,000	150.00
In estates 65,001 to $200,000	3/10 of 1% but not less than $300.
In estates over $200,001	*4/10 of 1% not not less than $400.

Note: The above list is not all inclusive but merely highlights some current Surrogate fees.

2. *Property Checklist*

ITEM	VALUE $$
Real Property	
Residence	
Business	
Personal Property	
Stocks	
Bonds	
Mutual Funds	
Savings Account	
Checking Account	
Furniture	
Automobile	
Personal Effects	
Business	
Proprietorship	
Partnership	
Corporation	
Insurance	
Personal	
Group	
Retirement	
Pension	
Profit Sharing	
Keogh	
IRA	
TOTAL =	$

3. Lawyer Referral Services

COUNTY	PHONE NUMBER:
Atlantic County	(609) 345-3444
Bergen County	(609) 488-0044
Burlington County	(609) 261-4862
Camden County	(856) 964-4520
Cape May	(609) 463-0313
Cumberland County	(856) 692-6207
Essex County	(973) 622-6207
Gloucester County	(856) 848-4589
Hudson County	(201) 789-2727
Hunterdon County	(908) 735-2611
Mercer County	(609) 585-6200
Middlesex County	(732) 828-0053
Monmouth County	(732) 431-5544
Morris/Sussex County	(973) 267-5882
Ocean County	(732) 240-3666
Passaic County	(973) 278-9223
Salem County	(856) 935-5629
Somerset County	(908) 685-2323
Sussex County	See Morris County reference above.
Union County	(908) 353-4715
Warren County	(908) 637-8055

4. Glossary

Account
A written document which a personal representative gives. It is a detailed financial history of the estate.

Acknowledgment
A certification by a notary public or New Jersey attorney that a person who signs a written document is indeed the person who signs it and acknowledges that this is the document he or she signs.

Administrator
The general administrator of an estate in which the decedent dies intestate (without a will). An administratrix is a female administrator.

Affidavit
A statement under oath. The person who signs swears that it is true. A notary or New Jersey attorney takes his or her signature.

Attestation Clause
A clause under which witnesses to a will signed. It declares that the will was signed, published and declared by the person signing it to be his or her last will, that it was signed in the presence of each of the witnesses, that they were present at the same time, that they, upon his or her request and in the presence of the person signing the will and in the presence of each other have signed it as witnesses. This is a perfect attestation clause. It permits probate of a will in common form upon the affidavit of only one of the witnesses.

Augmented Estate	No matter what the will says the surviving spouse may elect to take one third of what is known as the decedent's augmented estate. This is the value of the decedent's estate after certain items are subtracted from it and certain items are added to it.
Beneficiary	A person who receives a benefit in money or property under a will, insurance policy, bank account, employment plan, etc.
Caveat	A written document which protests the validity of an alleged will. To be effective a caveat is filed in the Surrogate's office before a will is presented for probate.
Codicil	A supplement or addition to a will which affects provisions in the will. A codicil is signed and witnessed the same way a will is.
Commissions	The compensation to a personal representative, trustee or guardian for services performed in administering an estate or trust. Commissions are generally authorized by New Jersey Statute.
Complaint	A written legal pleading. In New Jersey a civil action is started upon the filing of a complaint with the court.
Corpus	The principal sum or capital as distinguished from the interest or the income.

Curtesy	The surviving husband's right to take a one half life estate interest in his deceased wife's real property. The right of curtesy was abolished on and after May 28, 1980.
Decedent	The person who dies - also known as the deceased.
Devise	A disposition under a will of real or personal property. When devise is used as a verb, it means to dispose of real or personal property by will.
Devisee	Any person designated in a will to receive a devise.
Disclaimer	The renunciation of the right to receive property by way of will or gift or otherwise by an heir, beneficiary or other such recipient.
Donee	A person who receives a gift.
Donor	The person who makes a gift.
Dower	The surviving wife's right to take a one half life estate interest in her deceased husband's real property. The right of curtesy was abolished on and after May 28, 1980.
Estate	The property owned by a person. This can be real property or personal property. More specifically, it means the decedent's property which is subject to administration under the laws of New Jersey.

Executor	The administrator of the estate of a person who dies with a will. An executrix is a female executor.
Fiduciary	This generally includes an executor, executrix, administrator, administratrix, trustee and guardian (and others not discussed in this book).
General Legacy	A devise of personal property which is not specifically identified by the testator/ testatrix as a part of his/her estate. An example would be a residuary legacy. (See definition of residue below).
Guardian	A person who has been formally qualified by the court to take care of the person and/or manage the property of a minor or mental incompetent.
Guardian Ad Litem	A guardian appointed by the court to represent a minor or mental incompetent during the course of a particular civil action, such as the administration of an estate.
Heir	A person, including the surviving spouse, who is entitled to the property of a decedent who dies intestate (without a will).
Holographic Will	A will generally in the handwriting of the person who makes it and signed by him or her. Such a will does not conform to the statutory requirements. However, it can be a valid will. It may be admitted to probate only in solemn form in accordance with the court Rules.

In Kind	Property in an estate which is not cash.
Intangible Personal Property	Personal property which is not able to be felt or touched. This would be a bank account or a security, etc.
Interested Persons	All persons who do or might have an interest in an estate. These would include the beneficiaries under a will. These would also include the spouse, heirs, next of kin.
Intestate	When a person dies without a will it is said he or she dies intestate. An intestate estate is the estate of a person who dies without a will.
Inter Vivos	Literally, this means between the living. An inter vivos transfer is one in which property passes during lifetime. A testamentary transfer is when property passes under a will at death. An inter vivos trust is a trust which is established during the life of the testator and not under his or her will. A testamentary trust is a trust which is established under a will.
Issue	All of a person's lineal decedents, natural or adopted, of all generations.
Joint Tenancy With Right of Survivorship	Ownership by two or more persons. When one person dies his or her interest automatically passes outside the will to the surviving person(s). This is distinguished from tenancy in common (see below).

Legacy	A disposition of property by will. Technically, legacy is supposed to mean tangible personal property. It is loosely used to usually mean any personal property. Legacy has also been interpreted to mean essentially the same thing as a devise. For a general legacy, see General Legacy. For a specific legacy, see Specific Legacy.
Letters of Administration	A written document issued by the court which is evidence that the person receiving it has the right to administer an intestate estate (where the decedent dies without a will).
Letters Testamentary	A written document issued by the court which is evidence that the person receiving it has the right to administer a testate estate (where the decedent dies with a will).
Minor	A person who is under 18 years of age.
Next of Kin	The surviving spouse and the blood relatives (including those who have been adopted). These would be the parents, children, brothers and sisters, aunts and uncles, nieces and nephews, cousins, etc.
Personal Representative	The executor, administrator.
Post Mortem Estate Planning	Estate planning after the decedent's death and during the course of the administration of his or her estate for the purpose of minimizing taxes and adjusting rights and liabilities of parties.

Power of Appointment	A power or authority which one person gives to another in a will or other document. The person who receives the power of appointment is to receive property from the person giving it. He or she has the right in turn to appoint or select those person(s) who shall receive the property when a certain event such as death or the expiration of a period of time expires.
Power of Attorney	A written document which one person gives to another authorizing him or her to act on his or her behalf and be his or her agent. An agent is also known as an attorney-in-fact.
Principal	The principal sum or capital as distinguished from the interest or the income. Also known as corpus.
Probate	The act or process of proving that a decedent's will is in fact his or her will. Admitting a will to probate means that the will becomes a formal document of record and governs the disposition of the decedent's estate.
Probate in Common Form	Admission to probate of a will without a formal court hearing and upon the presentation of a self-proved will or the affidavit of one of the witnesses (if there is a perfect attestation clause).

Probate Estate	The decedent's estate which is subject to administration and which does not pass outside the estate directly to named beneficiaries as would happen with a joint bank account with right of survivorship or an insurance policy with a named beneficiary.
Probate in Solemn Form	This is a formal court proceeding. This takes place if a holographic will is offered for probate or a will is contested.
Refunding and Release Bond	A written document which a beneficiary or heir signs when he or she receives a distribution from the decedent's estate. This document releases the personal representative and agrees that in the event the estate incurs further liability, the person receiving the property will pay back all or part of it to satisfy such liability.
Renunciation	The voluntary surrender of a right or power, such as the right to serve as executor of an estate.
Residue	That part of the decedent's estate which is disposed of as the rest and remainder of the decedent's estate after the payment of debts and distribution of particular devises and legacies. The residue is disposed of in accordance with that clause of the will known as the residuary clause.

Self-Proved Will	When the decedent has signed the will in the presence of two witnesses and a notary public or a New Jersey Attorney has taken the signatures of all three. A particular form must be used.
Signature Guarantee	A written guarantee issued by a bank or brokerage house which guarantees a person's signature on a document. This is different from an oath or acknowledgment taken by a notary.
Specific Legacy	A devise under a will of a specific article of property or a particular fund or percentage or fractional share of such particular fund.
Stock Power	A written document which authorizes the sale of a security. The person who signs it is usually required to have his or her signature guaranteed.
Superior Court	A court of general jurisdiction in New Jersey. This court hears and decides all issues regarding wills, trusts and estates. It also has full authority over fiduciary accounts and other such things. It also has the jurisdiction to hear disputes or doubts arising before the Surrogate and to review any judgment by the Surrogate.
Surrogate's Court	There is one in each county. The Surrogate is a court officer who takes care of the probate of wills, the administration of estates and other related matters.

Tangible Personal Property	Property which has the ability to be touched. Like a car or a piano or furniture or jewelry. Distinguished from intangible property.
Tenancy by the Entirety	Joint tenancy with right of survivorship except that the people who own it are husband and wife.
Tenancy in Common	Ownership of property by two or more persons. When one person dies his or her interest does not automatically pass outside the will to the surviving person(s). Instead the interest of the person who dies passes through his or her estate and is distributed in accordance with his or her will or under the laws of intestacy in the event he/she dies without a will.
Testamentary	A testamentary disposition is a disposition by will and one that is not made during life (as opposed to an inter vivos disposition). A testamentary trust is a trust which is established and set forth in a will.
Testate	When a person dies with a will it is said he or she dies testate. A testate estate is the estate of a person who dies with a will.
Testator	The person who makes and signs a will.
Transferor	The person who transfers property to a person who is known as a transferee.

Transferee	A person who receives property transferred from a person who is a transferor.
Ward	A minor or mental incompetent placed by the court under the care of a guardian.
Waste	The destructive use of property causing it to lose value. Not taking care of a house can be waste. So can not taking care of money.
Will	This means the last will and testament of a testator and it includes any codicil.

ABOUT THE AUTHOR

Robert G. Saliba has been a New Jersey lawyer since 1966. His practice, which concentrates in estates, is in Morristown.

He is a graduate of Wesleyan University and Cornell Law School. In addition to this book, he has also written Administrative and Operational Trust Provisions, <u>New Jersey Transaction Guide</u>, Matthew Bender, and <u>Settling New Jersey Estates</u> (self-published).